ERMA

ERMA

*Erma Calderon with
Leonard Ray Teel*

RANDOM HOUSE
NEW YORK

Library of Congress Cataloging in Publication Data

Calderon, Erma.
Erma.

1. Calderon, Erma. 2. Afro-Americans—Biography.
3. Afro-Americans—South Carolina—Pinkney Island—
Biography. 4. Pinkney Island (S.C.)—Biography.
I. Teel, Leonard Ray. II. Title.
E185.97.C24A33 1981   973'.0496073   81–2774
ISBN 0–394–51743–1   AACR2

Manufactured in the United States of America

24689753

FIRST EDITION

I think Mrs. Knopf knows more than
anybody. Because she and I, we sat down and
talked quite a bit.

. . . And Mrs. Barker—I don't think anybody in the world has ever been told that
"I love you" as much as she told me.

—Erma

Preface

"You look exactly like I imagined you would be. Exactly." Mrs. Erma Calderon greeted me on a warm morning in April, 1977, when we met at the gate to her house in Bluffton, South Carolina. That day's journey to her birthplace in Allendale was the beginning of a lasting, deepening relationship. She spoke nonstop that day, and I stopped to buy more tapes for my recorder, and she filled those, too. As Mrs. Helen Knopf had told me beforehand, Mrs. Calderon spoke with clarity. Whether she was recalling an event of six years or sixty years ago, there were no important contradictions or failures of memory, and the story came forth from a natural storyteller.

We kept up this dialogue long-distance for four years, exchanging letters, tapes and telephone calls. The result is this oral autobiography of a self-taught Southern black woman who, shaped by dominant family ties and traditions, struggled from the age of nine years to manage her own life: first in the South, then in New York and Philadelphia, and finally back in the South again—her true home.

LEONARD RAY TEEL

Atlanta, Georgia
December 13, 1980

Introduction

The great migration from the rural areas of the South to the swarming cities was well under way by 1912 when one of the youngest travelers, a child named Erma, arrived in the noise and hustle of the Union Passenger Depot on Savannah's west side. Erma was bundled in her mother's arms. She was newborn, two weeks old, when her mother and sister stepped down from a combination baggage and coach car in which the Southern Railway segregated black riders. Erma's mother, Laura Best Milledge, was then twenty-three years old; Erma's sister, Vinie, was five.

Savannah was the gateway for thousands leaving the countryside. Many went on connecting trains to the cities of the North and Midwest, but many others stayed there, especially if they could find work. Savannah was so many times busier than the town of Allendale, South Carolina, where Erma had been carried aboard the railway car a few hours earlier.

In leaving home, her mother made a bold move. Evidently, she had been thinking for some time about the idea of leaving, but the actual decision to move seems to have been somewhat rushed. The three of them left as soon as possible after Erma was born on September 13, 1912. Two weeks later her mother set out. She left behind the certainties of the community where she had lived all her life. At Erma's birth she was living in her parents' home; now she would be on her own.

The choice of Savannah was deliberate, and the move was meant to be permanent. Like many others who were drawn to the cities of the South and the North in the early years of the century, Laura Milledge was encouraged by stories sent home by earlier adventurers. Three sisters had made the journey before her; their letters told of excitement and opportunities. They had not returned to Allendale.

But Laura was unlike thousands of others who left the countryside after 1900 in that she had lined up some reasonable prospects in advance of taking the train. When she set foot on the platform in Savannah, she carried in her bag the addresses of two persons who she already knew could help her. Both were women, and either one might have met the family that day in late September. One was Laura's friend from Allendale, Pearl. She had married a Jones, and together with her husband, was making a living peddling vegetables on the streets of Savannah. Pearl Jones had reported that a small frame house was available to rent on her own block, uptown on the west side where many blacks lived. She had also reported a job opening in the kitchen at the Oglethorpe Club, the downtown meeting place for many of Savannah's elite, prospering businessmen. Such prospects, together with the young mother's determination to get out on her own, probably accounted for the timing of her journey to Savannah.

The second address in her bag was for a house on Lumber Street, downtown on the west side, not far from the river and the wharves. One of her three older sisters, Ida Best, had lived there since leaving Allendale; like the other two, Ida had not married and had no children. Her two oldest sisters, Effie and Elizabeth (called Eliza), had gone on to New York City. Both had kept in touch with the family and on occasion, Eliza, the oldest, sent money home. Effie had settled in Brooklyn. Eliza had found a niche in Harlem, where she was said to be earning good money from her own beauty parlors.

The Best women were strikingly attractive. Exactly what proportions of black and white and Indian blood flowed in their veins, nobody was quite clear about. Erma simply would conclude that "the family was all mixed up." Her older cousin, Rebecca, daughter of one of the Best boys who had married a woman with blue eyes, explained the inheritance: "We're white—half white and half Indians. And I've got some sisters real white. But they're mixed. You understand." The American Indian contribution was undeniable in some of the women. Rebecca inherited Asiatic eyes. Indian features were pronounced in Eliza. Erma thought Eliza had more Indian blood than anyone in the family. The two long braids of jet-black hair hanging to her hips made her look still more Indian.

All of the Best girls had been particularly noticeable in Allendale because of their long hair. Effie had so much hair, Erma remembered, that she could never wear a cap. With various styles, it was possible to puff up their hair on top of their heads to an impressive height. On at least one occasion, the girls' hairstyle prompted some idle boys in Allendale to chase them, as Erma heard the story:

There were three or four white boys up on the corner one day. The ladies used to wear rats in their hair to make their hair look big. And they caught them and took their hair down, saying, "Those Best girls—that can't be their hair." You know how the ladies used to wear their hair puffed up on their head. And they took all the hair down. And my grandfather was so angry he went to this man's house. Got their sons in and said, "Did you take the Best girls' hair down?" "Well, we just didn't believe those girls had that much hair." Well, they tore them up. They were seventeen years old, but they got torn up.

The youngest of the Best women, Laura, had gray eyes, a light complexion, freckles and red hair. At twenty-three she wore her red hair shoulder-length. When she showed up at the door of the Oglethorpe Club, she made a good first impression. Her appearance, that of an attractive black woman who could pass for white, was no hindrance to her getting an audience for her talents in the kitchen. The club men were soon to benefit from the lessons Laura had learned in her mother's immaculate kitchen.

Laura's mother, Vinie, had been naturally upset when she left Allendale. Although she was twenty-three, she was still thought of as the baby girl. The parting must have caused her mother to think of Eliza and Effie and Ida. They had all taken the train, all left on the railway that was visible from the front porch of their house at 734 Railroad Avenue. The railroad tracks, two sets of rails, and Allendale's whitewashed depot had been an everyday sight all their lives. One by one they took the train to the world beyond.

All of the Best women had been born in the small frame house on Railroad Avenue, where Erma was born in September, 1912. Erma learned from her aunts years later that a midwife came and sat with her mother until the time arrived. Then a doctor was summoned.

The only problem for Laura appears to have been her husband, Allen Milledge. He had a reputation for being deathly afraid of the dark. His apprehension of the night made him somewhat useless when it appeared that Erma was going to be born before dawn, and he balked at going in the dark to get a doctor. This was apparently one of the final episodes of the marriage. Whatever other differences existed between Laura and Allen, they soon parted. Days after Erma was born,

Allen left town. He may already have taken to drinking in excess, which brought out a mean streak of beastly proportions. Whatever the case, he had evidently been cheating on Laura, at least during the final months of her pregnancy. He cast his lot with her best friend in town, a woman named Ella, and it was with Ella that he left Allendale. Years later Erma was told that the couple took one of the Southern Railway trains out of that whitewashed depot, headed toward Savannah. Her mother never mentioned his name. For nine years all Erma knew about her father was what her mother told her in a simple, unelaborated explanation: "Your father is in heaven." It was something that Erma could tell the children on Kline Street when they talked about their own fathers.

The breakup of the marriage, the general encouragement from her sisters and the promise of a job and a house—all contributed to Laura's decision to go to the city. Whatever her mother might have said to discourage her, or delay her, Laura left.

The final goodbyes were said at the old depot. Its overhang shaded the platform, where everyone probably stood until the time came to go down the wooden steps to the tracks. The engineer of the local train stopped if he saw the red flag hung out.

Before the train pulled in, there was a warm, probably tearful parting. Her parents, Carroll and Vinie, and Laura's three brothers would have been there. Angus, Thomas and Carroll made their livings in Allendale. Angus was successful in farming, sometimes hiring as many as two or three hundred men in a season to help in the planting and harvesting. He also had a sideline in the undertaking business. Angus Best's hearse, decorated with Biblical angels and pulled by a slow horse, was a familiar sight on the streets. Angus may have mentioned the gift he was arranging for Laura's new place in Savannah: a black chrome-trimmed stove. The middle brother, Thomas, was also a businessman, operating a shoe-repair business. He may have brought to the depot some of his children (eventually he had thirteen), one of whom, Rebecca, was soon to become a schoolteacher in Allendale.

Laura had every possible assistance from her family. Of all the girls, she had perhaps been the most obedient to her mother, and she was dearly loved. She was the only Best woman leaving Allendale with children. Her mother wanted her to take two family treasures. One was the baby grand piano which Laura played by ear, accompanying herself as she sang in an untrained but beautiful voice. The other gift was a four-poster bed with a handmade canopy. The family arranged to freight her belongings and the bed and piano after she was sure of a place to stay.

They would naturally have told her to come back if her plans did not work out. They at least expected her to come back with the children for a visit. They all hoped that she would keep in touch more closely than the other sisters. In fact, Laura did return, if only for the funerals of her mother and father and others. In Savannah, she would be near her sister Ida. Angus, the eldest and most generous of brothers, would remain reliable whatever the distance.

The mother and her two children may have been the only riders going to the end of the line on the local train. The locals generally carried commuters going to the next town to shop or do business and return. These locals were the only passenger trains that stopped in Allendale as a rule. A local engineer might stop even between towns, might halt in the middle of nowhere to pick up a fisherman hailing him from the side of the tracks so that he could go to the next fishing hole, where his luck might be better. The fare was about two cents a mile, but everyone paid the minimum ten cents. To Savannah, about seventy miles from Allendale, the ride would have cost $2.80 for Laura and Vinie. Erma likely rode at a cut rate, if not free.

From Allendale to Savannah the tracks went in almost a

straight line south. As schedules were generally set, the local train went to Savannah in the morning and made the return in the afternoon. When Jim Crow laws flourished, these trains carried two passenger coaches. One was for whites; the other was called a "combo"—combination half for baggage and half for blacks. There was no dining car on the local trains, so Laura had to pack whatever meal she and Vinie would eat before they got to Savannah.

Laura looked out on much the same scenery that Erma would see from a train window during her own voluntary migration sixteen years later: "Little shiny houses by the tracks. Most were poor blacks. Some were poor whites. Cotton and the peanuts and the cattle." Just north of Savannah the Southern Railway tracks crossed the muddy Savannah River on a trestle of graceful brick arches. The family was in Georgia.

Savannah in 1912 was a growing city with a hundred times more people than the town of Allendale. It was an old city that was being reshaped in the mold of a modern marketing and shipping center, with mechanized industry and commerce. The Southern Railway was one of four major lines and eight short lines that led into the city. Rail terminals and yards on both the east and west sides handled dozens of passenger and freight trains daily from every direction except east. To the east, eighteen miles down the Savannah River, passenger steamers and freighters entered the river channel from the ocean. The steamers regularly carried passengers between Savannah and Baltimore, New York and Boston, sometimes more cheaply than the railroads. Savannah's protected river harbor had been improved in recent years and had four miles of wharves. Many of the people who lived in Ida's neighborhood worked on the wharves, unloading and loading the freighters docked alongside the boxcars. Longshoremen worked through the night transferring Savannah's notable exports to the cargo holds, filling the ships with naval supplies, cotton, fertilizers and lumber. Such business was making small fortunes for some of Savannah's enterprising white merchant class.

The city had no shortage of labor. The population had swollen dramatically between 1890 and 1910. Between each decade the census showed a twenty-percent increase in population. As the migration from the country continued, and more blacks arrived, Savannah's established black population was joined by almost as many newcomers. Blacks outnumbered whites in the 1900 census (28,090 of the total 54,244).

The new arrivals generally doubled up with friends and families who had come ahead. Others struggled in the streets until they found shelter, increasingly turning to a new breed of enterprising landlords who quickly erected one-room windowless shacks between other larger shacks, all of them fronting on alleys behind the frame houses of the neighborhoods. One such neighborhood was where Ida lived, in Yamacraw, named after the Indians the British had found there in the 1730s. Yamacraw had been started before the Civil War as an outlying settlement for black freedmen. By 1912 the community had become a slum, a haven for the poor who crowded the shacks in the teeming alleyways not far from Ira's more comfortable rented house.

Erma's mother got off the train in a Savannah that was strictly segregated. Any relaxation of the Jim Crow laws was rare. The one segregationist idea which had not worked was the one for providing separate streetcars for each race. It was too expensive, since not enough whites rode the whites-only cars. The solution was to paint a white line after the first six rows of seats. Erma grew up riding the white-lined cars in which the rule was strictly enforced regardless of the absence of whites. On the west-side line on West Broad Street, Erma would see "always more blacks than whites . . . The whole front would be empty and yet people would stand up and sweat."

Earlier resistance by blacks to the Jim Crow laws had become muted by 1912, and most simply obeyed. The early defiance was past; the last of the streetcar boycotts had been in 1906. By the time Erma was brought to the city, segregation practices were literally spelled out all over town. There was a constant need to spell out the law because of the influx of new people from the country. Of course, the city was too large for every white person to know every black person, as was the case in towns like Allendale. In Savannah, those who could afford it invested in Goette's Savannah City Directory, which identified citizens by trade as well as race, noting who was *not* white by inserting, directly after the name, a small italic *c*.

Erma would grow up remarkably oblivious of this systematic racism. Yet she would remember the time she was rebuked for using the wrong water fountain at the five-and-ten. "Can't you read? Niggers don't drink here," she remembered being scolded by an angry woman. Erma's mother helped her daughters cope with this blatant brand of segregation. She told her daughters, "Who knows what color *love* is?"

In every respect Savannah must have made a keen impression on the young mother as she stepped out of Union Passenger Depot onto West Broad Street. Possibly accompanied by Pearl Jones, Laura may have hired one of the horse hacks whose black drivers waited for fares outside the doors of the depot. Most likely they first went to Pearl's house so that Laura could see the place that was available to rent.

Along the length of West Broad Street the horse hack drivers jockeyed among the new automobiles and the clanging streetcars. The horses were relics of the last century up against the mechanized marvels of the new era. Livery stables were fast disappearing from downtown Savannah, but the hacks were still the only cabs of their day and were frequently hired by people who had no car and had too much to carry on a streetcar. Photographs of the period before 1920 show West Broad Street's mix of old and new. Streetcars ran on tracks up the center of the street. Mules and horses hauled wagons loaded with deliveries of fruits and produce for the shops. Automobile drivers weaved around beasts and trolleys. Erma grew up hearing streetcar conductors clanging warnings to get off the tracks. Traffic accidents were not uncommon.

West Broad Street in 1912 was a meeting place of whites and blacks. The extensive commerce along the street, particularly downtown, brought them together during the daylight hours—the whites coming from the neighborhoods east of West Broad, and the blacks from those to the west. Some blacks lived in the white neighborhoods, particularly those who served as butlers. West Broad itself, the busiest thoroughfare on the west side, was a mixed residential street where moderately priced housing attracted tradesmen and professionals, pilots of steamboats, doctors and boilermakers, policemen and widows, blacks, whites and Chinese.

Kline Street was located well uptown, two blocks from West Broad. About thirty blocks from the waterfront, Kline Street was part of a black community that was growing quickly but with far more dignity and more plumbing than Yamacraw. As the demand for housing increased, landlords secured an extension of Kline Street to the Ogeechee Road, where it could not be extended any farther because of the Laurel Grove Cemetery. Beyond the cemetery were the city limits.

Arriving in the 800 block of Kline Street, Erma's mother saw a row of small one-story frame houses. They were owned by a single landlord who had painted them all gray, his color. Other landlords on other blocks signified their properties with personal colors: yellow or blue or red or green or dull rose. And all of the houses on all of the blocks in this part of

Savannah were enhanced by the cultivation of flowers, which seemed always to be blooming. Erma would remember them as "the most beautiful flowers . . . You could smell them before you got to the house." The baby bundled in her mother's arms lived here until she was six.

L. R. T.

ERMA

Introducing Erma's family.

My mother's name was Laura Milledge. She was real light.
Red hair, freckles. Very heavy bust, large bust like I have,
and tiny little waist. You know, those days they wore corsets.
And I remember me getting in the back of my mother and
lacing this thing up and tying it. And I don't know how they
breathed, but this is what they wore.

At 807 Kline Street, we lived there longer than we ever lived
anywhere, because I was a baby when my mother took me
there. When I was two years old, Catherine was born, by a
different father—because as far as I knew, my father . . . I
never had a father, you see, I was always told he was in
heaven. Catherine's father was John Henry Ashe. He was
mixed—black and white—and he was what you call a first-
class carpenter. There's homes in Savannah right now that he
built. My sister knew where they are, but I didn't. He was a
first-class carpenter: John Henry Ashe.

3

Home and Sunday School.

In my days when I was a child, Savannah was nothing but flowers—all kind of flowers, all kinds of beautiful flowers. You know, the flowers nowadays don't have . . . you don't smell them, you don't smell anything. But those days the flowers had the most beautiful . . . oh, you could smell them before you got near the houses. And everyone tried to outdo the other. Every house.

The first house that we lived in when we came to Savannah, it was 807 Kline Street, right off the Ogeechee Road. I know exactly where it is. Well, the Jews owned all of the houses—all of them—and we only paid eight dollars a month. Everybody paid eight dollars a month. Well, it was hard to get eight dollars a month those days. My mother made very good money according to what the other women made those days.

The man that we rented from, all of his homes, you could always tell—each landlord had his own color—his were gray. Another landlord, his homes would be yellow. Some would be blue, some would be red, some would be green and some would be a dull, dead-looking rose color.

They all looked alike. They were all joined on together. And they had what you call a little bench, and it was a stoop—it wasn't a porch. But they were scrubbed with lye until they were yellow. They were beautiful. You could eat off the floor.

My mother was spotless. And we had to be the same way. We washed our socks and our hair ribbon every day. They were washed, and the ribbon was ironed. The socks were put up to dry. And that dress . . . the dresses that we wore was hung up. And you better not see anything on that dress but just the little crease, you know, where you sat down. And that was hung up, and the next day we put on another dress, and for five days we changed our dresses, and then we'd go back the next week to the first dress that we had on before.

Now, when we came home from school, the shoes had to come off. Those shoes had to be put away. We had shoes that we wore to school and we had shoes that we wore to church.

And we used to have Sunday School cards with a lesson on it. And when we went to Sunday School—this was for the children; the adults didn't go—you had to come back and explain everything that you learned in Sunday School. They'd take that card, and just held that card, and you'd better know that lesson. And I learned my prayers and I learned everything that I know from the Bible from my mother's knees. She was very old-fashioned, but very wise, a very wise woman. I mean she used to take us to her—one knee and one knee—and teach us.

And about reading and writing—I taught myself. The only thing I knew, I knew how to count to a hundred. And I knew my alphabets. My mother taught me that before I went to school. But the rest of it—I taught myself.

The Oglethorpe Club.

My mother was working at the Oglethorpe Club in Savannah, Georgia. It's still there. It's a place that the wealthy people would hire for weddings and big dinners and banquets. And when they got through with the food that they had, they didn't want it. The help got it. And my mother used to feed the whole neighborhood.

Those days they had open trolley cars—they were yellow. And if the weather was all right, you were safe. But if it rained, shame on you. And then, instead of a taxi, they had the hacks with the horse. If the food was enough to put in a bag, she would take the trolley. If it was too much for that, she'd get a hack. And she would come home loaded down and she fed the whole neighborhood.

She went to work at six o'clock in the morning, and she would come home at three, bringing the food. And then she would go back and come home at eleven o'clock at night, right on time.

My poor mother, I remember in the winter time when she would come home from work. And we didn't have any hot-water bottle or any electric pad or anything. We used to take the bricks and put them in the fireplace and get the bricks hot. And we'd take those bricks and go all over that bed and get that bed just as nice and warm as toast. When she'd come home, that bed would be so nice and warm. I think about all those things—how people have it now, how convenient everything is. All you have to do is turn on the electric blanket.

About the Oglethorpe Club. Oh, I never saw any of the rooms. My mother worked in the pantry. She did all of the pastry work and all of the salads. She never complained about her problems. She loved her job. She had to, because she worked there from the time that she came to Savannah—I was two weeks old, I think—and she worked there up until she died. That's the only job she ever had. No, we weren't allowed to go into the club—just the kitchen and the pantry, which was about twice the size of my little house here. They had the first cook, the second cook and the chef.

I think most of the men smoked cigars. I saw that in the trash on the outside. I never went in there to see, but as I said, I saw the trash that was being brought out. I saw bottles that whiskey was in.

*Erma's mother teaches a lesson in crime and
punishment.*

One day my mother took my sister and I—I think we were
going to her job, yes. Well, and we saw these men, and they
had these funny-looking uniforms on. They were black and
white, but they were round—they weren't striped up and
down, they were round. And little hats that were made the
same way. And they had these long chains. They were
shackled to each one of their legs. And they had this great big
ball. Well, what in the world? Momma, what is that? Why
are all those men dressed like that? And why do they have the
chains around their legs? How can they walk? They can't go
but so far?

My mother was always the type that never nothing
interfered with her explaining every question that we asked
her. Even if we had guests. Everything was always explained
to us. So she told us that these men had broken the law, and
they were being punished.

"Well, how—what do you mean?"

"Well, they're disgraced. They're digging ditches out

there. Their friends see them. And this is what you call 'working on the chain gang.' "

"Well, where is the chain gang?"

"That's the chain gang."

"I don't see any chain gang."

"The chains around their legs and their ankles. And that big ball—they can go so far and no more."

"Well, why is the man, why does the man have that great big gun?"

"If they attempt to run, he will shoot them."

"Well, how can they run with the big—with that big ball? How can they run with the chains?"

"Some of them get away."

Well, that stayed with me all day, and I worried my mother and I talked to her. So when we went home that night she just sat me down and explained, and told me: "Erma, when you break the law, you have to be punished. Just like God's law. When we break God's law, he punishes us. Not *that* way. But we're punished."

"So now these men have to go around all of their lives with this—"

"No, darling. They have a certain number of years that they are sentenced."

So I began to cry.

"Erma, why are you crying?"

"I feel so— Those poor men, I feel so sorry for those poor men. When they go back to the— You said they go back to the house?"

"The prison, yes."

"And then they're gonna be shot."

"No, Erma. When they go back to the prison, there is a man that's called the warden. He's over everybody."

"Even . . . even those old bad men with the guns?"

She said yes. "He is the boss. And what he says goes."

"Oh! Well, do they take the chains off them when they go home?"

9

"Yes. Now remember, the warden is the one that's over everybody. And when these men go back, they're treated like anybody else. They get a lot of food to eat."

"Like, what do they get?"

She says, "Black-eyed peas and rice and cornbread."

I says, "Well then, what do they get the next day?"

"Well, lima beans and rice and cornbread."

I says, "Well, they don't ever get anything, no different things to eat?"

"Oh, Christmas," she says, "they have, uh, they have turkey dinners. Or stewed chicken. They have stewed chicken or something like that. Pork chops."

I still cried.

"Erma," she says, "you know something? You really should be a minister. If I ever saw a woman that needed to be a minister, you should be. You feel sorry for everybody. You can't make a nurse because you're . . . you're too easy-hearted. But, my darling, you cannot take on the world."

"So the man that's over all of these people, and what he says goes, that's the warden?"

"That's the warden."

"All right."

Erma finds an appropriate nickname for her mother.

We had a great big black range. It was a huge thing, but it was beautiful. Most of the people they just cooked from a fire. Not my mother. My mother's stove had to be as clean as her table, and that was my job, to do that stove every Friday. It was polished with black polish—black polish—and rubbed down with the skin of bacon, a piece of bacon skin, buffed and polished until it couldn't shine any more. And the chrome was cleaned also. Where the ashes went—your bread box couldn't be any cleaner. That box was taken outside and washed, rinsed out, dried, and inside it was clean. The oven— spotless. The top of the stove was what we called a warmer. When you cooked your food you put it up there. And on the side, it was for hot water.

And let me tell you something. My mother would come home and take a white piece of cloth and go over that stove. Now, that's my job, see. And I'm standing there, trembling, just shaking to death. If it was a spot on that cloth, that towel, you do it over tomorrow. So I told my sister, I said, "You know who Momma is?" She said, "Who?" I said she's the warden.

And we nicknamed her the warden. She heard us one day, but it was quite a while later. But I got wise. When I got through cleaning the stove, *I* would get a piece of white cloth and go *all* over it. And when she would come home I would have a beautiful piece of white cloth there for her to go over the stove, because I knew there wasn't nothing on it.

And our pots hung. We didn't have the pegboards like you have now. Just the nails. Every pot hung on the wall, and every pot was as clean as it was the day it was bought. In those days the bottom part of the house was wood—I'm talking about the walls inside of the rooms. And the upper half, that was painted. Our woods were scrubbed twice a year. We didn't have tablecloths on our kitchen table. A lot of people had the oilcloth; my mother didn't want them. She was afraid of roaches. But that table, it was as pretty as anything you ever saw in your life. And the floors—they had no linoleum, nothing on our kitchen floor. The other rooms, yes, but not our kitchen floor. You could eat off it. You could drop anything and pick it up and eat it. It was scrubbed—every other day it was scrubbed. And we had what you call knotholes. She had a man to come by and—it was a good thing there was no snakes in Savannah, because we would all been dead—drill these holes in certain parts of the floor. And that floor was scrubbed, on our knees, with the lye and, uh—what was it she used?—ashes. And when we got through with that floor, we rinsed it, I mean we rinsed it, and the windows were open. Well, you didn't have to dry it because the waters went through the holes, see. The yard was spotless. *Underneath the house* had to be spotless. We never had tin cans or trash or anything in our yard. When she came home, she walked outside. If there was a matchstick in the yard—that was you. Of course, nobody smoked in our family.

So I called her the warden. I told her one day, I said, "Momma, you know, you are the warden, up to the prison." And it tickled her, so she never said anything about it. Never. She was such a sweet woman.

The story of Erma's older sister, Vinie, whose powers make the family afraid.

We were so happy there on 807 Kline Street. That's where my older sister Vinie died. That is the one that we were afraid of so much. There was something very strange about her and we didn't understand it. I still don't. She could tell you anything in the world that was gonna happen. Or if you lost something, she would tell you where to go and find it. And so many things that she would tell us until we were afraid of her.

Catherine and I would come to the house from the store or play, and we could hear these children—sound like it'd be thirty-five or forty children—laughing. You could hear them just laughing and playing. And we'd run to the door. Oh, somebody's got a lot of children in here. But when we opened the door—not a sound, everything was stopped. There would be no one in there but my older sister. And you could feel your skin crawling and the hair standing up on the top of your head. That happened several times, and one day we told Momma about it. Well, she knew before, because it had happened to her. And she was afraid. She didn't know what it was—she didn't know. She didn't understand Vinie. We were all afraid of her. My mother used to send her over to my Aunt Ida's to stay a lot. I don't know if she knew what it was all about or not.

But let me tell you about the Gypsies stealing Vinie—which was most of her fault too, because she went with them. They didn't have so much stealing to do, but they suggested it.

Vinie was fascinated about—oh, so was I, but I was afraid of them—about the bright colors that they wore.

Between Kline Street and Thirty-sixth Street, there was a big lot there—about a block, just open there. And the Gypsies, they camped there in huge wagons. To this day I have never seen such large wheels on wagons. The wagons were covered, because they took all their belongings in there, and it used to be a surprise how much merchandise they could get in those wagons. They had their stoves, which they cooked on outside most of the time. They made a fire right outside. But they had these little two-burner stoves—it was something like butane gas I think that they used. I don't know what it was. Anyway, if it rained too much, they would cook right inside the wagon.

And my mother was the type that had to feed the Army if you would let her. Well, as I said, we always had a plenty. One day we were sitting on the porch—stoop they called them because they were so small. And my mother was churning ice cream because she had made this beautiful cake. I think it was Vinie's birthday—yes, it was. And this little girl and two boys from the Gypsy camp, they stopped. And you know how children are—they stand there and they look.

And my mother said, "Go home and ask your mother can you have a piece of cake and some ice cream."

They said, "Yes."

"No," she says, "go home and ask your mother."

So the mother came back with them. Not only did the children have ice cream and cake, she did too, and wound up taking the rest of the cake, ended up taking the rest of the cake that was left. My mother gave it to her.

And the next day the children and the mother were back. And she told my mother, "This is a beautiful girl. What a beautiful girl, child." This was *Vinie*. Well, she was beautiful. She was jet-black, with coal-black hair just like the Indians in our family. Great big beautiful eyes and long eyelashes. They were the longest I think I've ever seen on anybody. She was beautiful.

And Vinie said to this woman, she says, "Why did you steal that pin?"

She says, "What pin?"

She says, "*That* pin. Why did you steal that pin?"

She said, "I didn't."

Then Vinie said, "Oh, yes you did. Yes you did." She said, "You went in the back door and stole that pin."

Well, the woman looked at Vinie. She says, "You're mistaken, little girl."

My mother said, "Her name is Vinie." She says, "Don't pay her any mind. She's always telling people things to get them upset. Vinie, why do you do this to me? Why, Vinie?"

The woman said, "I wish we had her."

My mother said, "Take her. I wish somebody would take her." You know, not *meaning* it.

And the woman went on back. And the next day she was there with an older woman, old gray-headed lady.

The woman said, "This is the child I was telling you about."

So Vinie looked at the old lady. She says, "She *did* steal that pin, you know."

The gray-headed lady said, "I don't think so, little girl."

Vinie says, "My name is Vinie."

The woman says to my mother, "Can she go home with us and play with the children?"

My mother said, "Yes, they can go."

So we all, we went. And this is when I saw, really saw,

this camp, and the beautiful dresses that they wore. The colors were just gorgeous, and they were real long, real long, down to the ankles, *all* colors. And they had—what do you call them?—tambourines, and they would play and the ladies would dance, and there was *one* girl that danced, you couldn't keep your eyes off of her. And I would cry for the violin. When they played the violin, I would actually cry. I'm like that today, I can't help it. There's something about a violin that really fascinates me.

And we would go, and they would come. And my mother got to the place that she would send a big dishpan full of food. Well, they would be there when she came home.

And Vinie did beautiful tatting—anything with a needle, she could do it. And she gave them some lace that she'd made.

And again this woman asked my mother—she was fascinated with Vinie. But we didn't know that she had planned to steal her.

So the lady next door said to my mother, said, "Laura, you're always criticizing Vinie," said, "But I believe that woman stole that pin."

My mother says, "Why would you say that?"

The lady said, "You know how Vinie is! That's what I'm telling you now." She said, "You better listen to some of the things that this child tells you. She's never said anything to any of us that wasn't true, and you know that."

My mother said, "That's what I'm afraid of."

She said, "Well, that woman stole that pin."

Momma said, "I don't think so. Vinie is letting her imagination run away with her."

She said, "I'm gonna tell you another thing. You better stop having those people come here, because they will steal everything that isn't nailed down." She says, "Now, Vinie told that woman that she stole that pin, and that woman stole that pin."

My mother says, "Don't let her hear you saying things like this. I don't want her to hear you saying this, because she really will believe these things herself." She said, "I think it's a little game with her."

She says, "Laura, you know you don't think any such thing."

So Momma told us—she did believe it, she believed it—and she told us, "I don't want you going over to the Gypsies any more. And if they come here looking for anything, we don't have it."

So about a week—no, about two weeks after that—the woman came back. But my mother had told her not to come back any more because we didn't have anything else to give.

So the woman asked could she see Vinie.

Momma says, "No. Vinie is in the house." Because when she saw her coming she made us go inside. Of course, me, I'm right to the window, you know, listening to everything that was going on.

And Vinie started to cry.

I said, "What's the matter?"

She said, "I *love* them. I like to see them, I like the music."

I said, "Me too. Momma don't want us to play with anybody that you can have any fun with."

So she says to me, she said, "When Momma goes to work—when she goes to work, I'm going over there." She says, "Because they say they're leaving. I'm going over and tell them goodbye." She said, "You won't tell Momma?"

I said, "Can I go too?"

She said, "No, you stay here. You stay home. And you can go tomorrow."

I said, "Well, they won't *be* here tomorrow."

"Well, I'm coming right back."

I waited and I waited and waited and waited—no Vinie.

When Momma came home—"Where's Vinie?"

"I don't know."

"Erma, where is Vinie?"

"I don't know."

Well, Catherine must have known. But she was off playing.

So when it began to get dark, I got a little afraid. I was afraid. I said, "Momma, Vinie went over to see the Gypsies this morning."

She says, "What!"

I said, "Vinie went over to see the Gypsies this morning."

She says, "Oh, my God." She says, "I'm gonna put it on her when she comes home. I'm going over there."

So she and the lady next door and the lady's husband, they went over there, and me—Catherine and I. And when we got there, the lot was clean. There was no wagon in sight. They were gone.

Well, my mother almost went crazy. She knew that they'd . . . that Vinie was with them. She wasn't gone long, they got her, I think it was four days, they found her. But they were in Americus, Georgia, when she was found. There's a place called Americus, Georgia, I will never forget it. And they lied, and said that Vinie followed them, they didn't know she was in the wagon. But Vinie says they told her to come on and go, they would bring her back. And I believe that's what happened. I don't believe that Vinie hid away in the wagons. I don't believe that. So it was their words against Vinie's, but anyhow, they found her and brought her back.

Momma told her, said, "If you ever—if either one of you ever—go out of this house into anybody's home or anywhere else," she said, "I'm gonna tear you up."

Well, you see, that was really Momma's fault, because she had no right feeding them or getting friendly with them. But that was my mother. She couldn't stand to see a hungry child look at her, or an adult. That's my Momma. That *was* my Momma.

Oh, but my mother did ask her again, she said, "Vinie, why did you say the Gypsy stole the pin?"

She says, "Because she did."

Momma said, "Why did you tell her that she went in the back?"

She says, "Because while the other Gypsies were talking to the lady in the front, she went in the back, and she stole that pin." She said, "Momma, you don't believe me."

But Momma said, "Yes, I believe you." Now, that's the first time I ever heard my mother admit to Vinie that she believed her about anything.

In those days when people was like my sister, they said they were witches. And we had people throw stones at our house, and she couldn't go to school, they would throw stones at her. She was in school one day and she went and she told the teacher, "You shouldn't have any class tomorrow." Teacher said, "Why?" "Because there's going to be a fire. Don't have any class tomorrow." Well, everyone knew about her, so it went through the whole school: no class tomorrow. And they *did* have a fire.

And then it got worse. It got worse, people began to shun the house and not come around because it was a witch there. Well, those days they believed in killing you or stoning you to death because you was a witch, you was evil. She wasn't evil. It was something—it was a gift that she had that we didn't understand.

Now, one of the ladies from the club that my mother worked for had given me a beautiful dress and a slip to go with it. She sent it back from Germany. And it was way too big—it would take me three or four years before I could wear it. And my sister Vinie wanted it. And my mother said, "Well, why don't you give it to Vinie, Erma, you will never wear it. It will be three or four or five years before you could wear that dress." It was about five years' difference between us. And one day we were sitting on the porch. This was on a Saturday—no, it was on a Friday. And she said to my mother, she said, "Momma," she says, "please don't slap me or don't laugh and make fun at me," she says, "but you know for the last week I have been seeing a white coffin in the front of the fireplace. So yesterday I went and looked in the coffin." She says, "What do you think was in that coffin?" My mother said, "I don't know." She said, "It was me. And I had on Erma's dress and slip." So we all looked at each other. My mother sat up all night, Catherine and I sleeping in her lap, half on the floor and half in her lap. Vinie went to bed.

And the next day Miss Gertrude Davis—she was a schoolteacher, she lived on Thirty-sixth Street in the house that we later moved in—she asked my mother could I come and spend the night with her. She wanted to adopt me. And my mother said yes. So I went on home with her. Oh, she had this gorgeous bathroom and everything. It was her father and her sister, Aunt Alma—each had their own bedroom, and I slept with her. Well, I have never been bathed and pampered and powdered and loved and hugged so much in my life. So about three o'clock in the morning—probably about eleven o'clock that night—a man came around there pounding on the door, ringing the bell, and he said to tell Miss Davis to come right away and bring me, bring Erma. "What is it?" He said Vinie is very sick. Well, Miss Davis knew about what Vinie had said; everybody knew about it. And we went on around there in our night clothes. It was just about a block away. And when we got there Vinie was dead. She was dead.

The undertaker's name was Monroe, and I think they're still in Savannah. My sister's name was Vinie Milledge. Vinie Arockerson Milledge. You can check it if you want to, because I still think the family's carrying on the business: Monroe, undertaker, on West Broad Street. They're still there. And I remember when they came to get Vinie. You know, in those days they put them in a basket. Catherine bit the man on his thigh—they almost dropped the body. Well, she and I was both fighting him like wildcats. They weren't going to take our sister away from us. Well, my mother had passed out. And the next day my mother said to me, she said, "Erma."

I said, "Yes, ma'am." She said, "You love your sister, don't you?" I said, "Yes, ma'am, I really love my sister. I love my sister and I want her to come back." She says, "Will you give her your dress and slip?" "Oh no, no way, uh-uh. I love her, but not that— That dress is going to stay for me until I can wear it." My mother didn't pay me any mind. She took my dress and slip and she buried her in it—just like Vinie *said* she saw herself in that coffin with that dress and slip on. And I'm glad she did, because I didn't have any sense then.

And to this day I can't understand my sister. Where did she get the knowledge? I told you about the lady next door losing her watch. And Vinie told her, she said, "Your watch wasn't lost. It was stolen. Your nephew stole it. And it's in the pawnshop on West Broad Street." She told her where to go, and that's where it was. And the lady said to my mother, "You will never raise her. She wasn't . . . she wasn't sent here to stay. You will never raise her." She was true. Vinie died at the age of fifteen.

Now, today you would call her—I don't know what you would call her—spiritualist, I imagine, but she was gifted. She was really gifted.

We went to the store one day to get a loaf of bread. Bread was five cents a loaf, and for supper we used to have the syrup and bread—that was all. Syrup and bread for supper, because at dinner time, at twelve o'clock, we had a big heavy meal. For supper, light—syrup and bread. And we loved it. And Vinie would get the bread and she would cut it in three pieces. They weren't great big loaves of bread like the ones we have here now. They were little small loaves of bread. And on the way back from the store Vinie said to me— my mother had a cousin or something, we called him Uncle Cap because he never wore anything but a cap—she says, "Look at Uncle Cap dancing on the top of the roof. Will you look at that?" And we didn't see nothing, my sister and I.

"Where?"

"Look over there."

I said, "Well, he doesn't live over there. He lives—"

She said, "He's going from one part of the roofs to the other."

See, the houses were joined all together.

"I don't see him."

"Well, *I* see him. Look how he's dancing."

I said, "Are you crazy? Uncle Cap is very, very sick."

She says, "Not any more. Because he's dancing."

And we took off. Catherine and I took off and left her walking. We had to pass the cemetery. That's where we were when she saw him. On Ogeechee Road. I think the name of the cemetery is Laurel Grove Cemetery.

We fell in the door. "What's the matter?"

"Momma, Vinie said Uncle Cap was dancing on the top of the roof."

She said, "Vinie is crazy." She said, "Uncle Cap is at the point of death."

When Vinie came in, Momma said, "Why do you want to frighten these children?"

"Momma," she said, "please don't slap me. Don't punish me. Uncle Cap is dead."

"What do you mean Uncle Cap is dead?"

"Momma, Uncle Cap is dead."

She says, "Young lady, you go to bed. Don't take a bath. Don't get any supper or nothing. Go to bed. I'm sick and tired of this," she says, "and you keep it up, I'm going to put you in a home someplace because I can't stand it. You're driving me, the children and the neighbors crazy."

"All right, Momma."

So Vinie went to bed. She didn't take a bath and she didn't get any supper. And after a while, about five minutes after Vinie went to bed, we heard this screaming and banging on the doors.

"Laura, *please* come. Laura, *please* come." And it was Uncle Cap's wife. She says, "Cap is dead. Cap's dead."

Then we *really* were afraid of Vinie. We were *really*

afraid of her. You see, we didn't know. We didn't know about people that could tell you things, or spirituals. She was born that way.

So my mother asked my Aunt Ida could my sister stay with her. She said, "Not me. No way. No way."

There was another lady that used to make doughnuts, and we loved her doughnuts. And she was crazy about Vinie. So she came over that evening. She says, "Can Vinie go home and spend the weekend with me?"

Momma said, "Of course. Any time." But other than that, she stayed home.

And I will swear before God in heaven about the children laughing and giggling. You could hear them—forty or fifty children just laughing and giggling. When you opened the door—bah, not a sound, not a child. You would see Vinie sometimes standing in the middle of the floor or sitting in the bed. And we'd say to her, "Where are the children? What happened to the children?" She says, "Do you see any children? You would have to come in and spoil everything, wouldn't you?"

And I—to this day—I never understood Vinie. Well, she died at the age of fifteen.

Introducing Mrs. Pearl Jones and her husband—
James Jones, nicknamed Papa Yellow.

Miss Pearl—what kind of a woman she was, she was very tall, straight, big-boned, no fat. She walked and stood as straight as an arrow. It was on account of the work that she did. I don't know whether you've ever seen this or heard of it before, but years ago in Savannah there was no vegetables in any of the stores, there was no such a thing as fresh vegetables. You had to go to the Farmers Market to get your vegetables. I'm so sorry they tore it down, I don't know what to do, because it was just gorgeous. They had everything in there that you wanted from the country, straight from and fresh from the country. Now it's a garage.

So the ladies used to have these great big baskets, they were handmade. They were the size of a big tin tub, but not quite as high, about the half, I would say. I would say they were about thirteen inches high and they were flat all but right in the center—they rose up just a little bit. And they would go out in the streets with these baskets on their head, with butter beans. And they had cardboard that would divide it, and they would always have more butter beans because the people down here ate more green butter beans than any other kind of beans or peas. And on the other side they would divide that and they would have like field peas or crowder peas or green peas—all shelled. And they had a pint-sized tin cup and a quart-sized tin cup.

And Miss Pearl would put that basket on her head, and what kept it up there I don't know. I don't know. It wouldn't fall off. She could stoop down and pick up a pin and that basket stayed on her head. Well, those days the women wore aprons, and she would take about five dollars' worth of change in her pocket and hit the street, out where the housewives were. And they had a regular little song that they would sing:

> "Get your beeeeeans,
> Butter beans!
> Green peas!
> Field peas!
> Beans, ladies!
> Beans, ladies!"

And sometimes before she could get four blocks, she wouldn't have a bean or a pea left. She would be sold out. Then she'd come back and stop by the Farmers Market and get a whole bushel of butter beans and put it in that basket and set it on the top of her head and come back home with those beans. Now, this was when we were living in Savannah, this was where my mother knew them—Mrs. Pearl and her husband.

She was about, I would say, a mahogany color. And Papa Yellow was jet-black. All of the children called him Papa because they both wanted children, and they loved children, and all of the children called him Papa. So one day somebody said, "You're so black, we're gonna call you yellow." So that was it, they called him Papa Yellow.

And *he* had what you call a pushcart. It had two wheels on it like a wagon wheel and a wheel in the front. Some people had two wheels and a big stick in the front to keep it from rolling, but he had a wheel in the front. And he took okra, tomatoes and string beans and corn, radishes, celery—everything that grew—asparagus and . . . what do you call the vegetables that the Italians are so fond of? Well, he had cauliflower. Every kind of vegetable that you can imagine was in that pushcart. And he would leave early in the morning, and he would go back by the market before they closed, and he would come back loaded down with peas and more beans—to shell.

Now, in the back of the store, in the back of the house, they had a little small room, and they had soda water and ice cream and candies. And they used to have this long black candy called licorice; it was made long like a strap, like a belt. The children loved it. I used to chew it too—make your teeth black, but I loved it. They had that, and they had a little—there was another candy that they sold—had a little tiny brown thing, one little dip was for a penny; they were peanuts covered with a red candy. And they were delicious; I loved those. And they had round peppermint bars, and they had pickles, ginger snaps and animal crackers and things like that.

And the children would come in every evening—sometime fifteen or twenty of them. And each child had a pan—they would bring their pans from home. And they'd sit up there and they would shell those peas and beans, and sometime within two hours there was nothing left to shell. And they would give each child twenty-five or thirty cents, which the children spent right there in the store before they went home. And that's the way they made their living.

Miss Pearl never had a chance to cook. And every evening that my mother came home, my sister and I would have to go up there with this basket of food. And she really was—I thought—my mother's dearest friend, because my mother never missed a day sending that food up there. Even on Saturdays—no, not Saturdays, because they worked on Saturdays. Even on *Sundays* she sent that food.

Erma plays games, is forbidden to play hide-and-go-seek at night and is spanked for playing Rock Aunt Dinah.

Oh, the games we played:

> *"Go round the rich man, tra-la-la-la.*
> *Go round the rich man, tra-la-la-la.*
> *Go round the rich man, tra-la-la-la.*
> *I, oh, love sugar and candy."*

Now, you see, all of the children were holding hands, and one boy or one girl would be in the ring, in the center. And then we would go around, we would say:

> *"Up the green valley,"*

You're still going around holding hands:

> *"Down the green valley,"*

The last one stoops down:

> *"Tell me, sweethearts."*

And the last one that was caught stooping down, *he* was put in the ring and he had to tell which girl he loved that was there, which girl he liked the best. And that went on till the game was over, till everyone had been picked. You understand?

And now—this is a game that I will never forget as long as I live. This was the one that when I got through getting a spanking with a hairbrush I couldn't sit down. It was called Rock Aunt Dinah. Now, all the children stood around. And a girl and a boy was put in the ring, and they sang:

"Rock Aunt Dinah, rock."

They're clapping their hands. They're not holding hands. The foot is going and the hands are clapping:

"Rock Aunt Dinah, rock,
Rock Aunt Dinah, rock Aunt Dinah,
rock Aunt Dinah, rock,
Rock Aunt Dinah, roll,
Rock Aunt Dinah.

Come on an' rock Aunt Dinah, rock,
Rock Aunt Dinah, rock,
Rock Aunt Dinah, rock Aunt Dinah,
rock Aunt Dinah, rock."

The same dances that they are doing today—the same identical dances that we did when we were children, they're doing them today. And no one could Rock Aunt Dinah like I could. Oh, my little butt was going up and down and around and around, between these two boys. So my mother called me. I didn't know she was peeping through the curtain. So when I came in she grabbed me. And she had this hairbrush. And when she got through with my little butt, it was blistered. No more Rock Aunt Dinah for me. And I tried to tell her they do it at the school and the teachers don't say anything.

"I don't care what they do or when they do it. No more Rock Aunt Dinah for you."

I said, "Well, Catherine does it."

She said, "I saw her. But she was just barely moving. But you are what you call 'shakin' that thing'—and you're never going to do it again. I'll *blister* you."

Okay. I never rocked Aunt Dinah any more.

And then there was another game that we played, that was hide-and-go-seek. A boy or girl would count up to a hundred and everybody had to go and hide. Well now, we could play it in the daytime, but my mother would not allow Catherine and I to play it at night. And I couldn't understand that. All of the children would play, and we had to sit on the porch, on the steps, until that game was over. Not at night—we couldn't play hide-and-seek. And you know, it took sometimes a half an hour to find those children. And sometimes the boys and girls would go and hide together. And as I grew older, I realized why we couldn't play hide-and-seek at night.

Well, that's the games.

And then we used to play jump rope. That's right. You would put the rope on the ground and you would step over it. And you would come back, and it would be a little higher. And you would come back and it would be a little *higher*. And the higher the rope was, the further you would go, you know, to come back to jump. And I've seen boys and girls *jump* as high as their height over a rope. And this is the same thing that they're doing now with a *pole*. So, you see, we invented these things years ago. This isn't something that's new, that just happened. And we did all kinds of tricks— which I saw on TV the other day—jumping the rope and skip rope. We did all kind of tricks inside the rope. We turned around. We faced each other. We danced together—

on that rope, while they were turning that rope, all kind of tricks—in that rope while it was jumping.

And of course, when it was raining, we played jackstones. We had twelve jacks and you played onesies, twosies, threesies, foursies, fivesies—till you got up to twelve. And it was fun— with a little rubber ball.

And those were the games that we played. Now, you didn't ask for that, but I told you.

Church picnics on Daufuskie Island.

There is one place that my mother used to take us to. The church would give a picnic, and we would go on the boat. The name of this place is called Daufuskie Island. Now that I have a little sense and know a little more than I did when I was a child, I'm just dying to get back over there, because I've been reading about this place. It's very popular. The people that's living there are just like they were hundreds of years ago. They say it's just like going to Africa. They are people set in their ways, they talk different, their religion is different. And from what I've been hearing about it, it's just amazing.

They have their own language. Now, it's supposed to be English, but you couldn't understand one word they say, because I met several people from there and I didn't know what they were saying.

You ask someone, Well, where is the broom, or where is the rake, or where is . . . ?

"Shawn de-ah."

Well, *shawn de-ah* means "See it there."

There's so much over there that I wish you could see. They say it's a beautiful place. I remember going there as a girl—oh, several times, at least eight or nine times, on picnics. But I did not know the value of the island. We never came in contact with any of the people that lived there.

I think they have one telephone, if I'm not mistaken, on the island. I don't think there's any more than one, and they *just* got that. And now that this island has been discovered— and these slaves, and ex-slaves, are living there—it has become very popular. Now, they say, people will be coming from all over to see it. Because, I was told, it was just like going into Africa.

The people, they speak—Gullah, I think is the name, the language that they speak. Gullah, or something like that. Well, I met several of them in the five-and-ten, and I kept following them around just to hear them talk, pretending to be shopping but listening to them. It was just fascinating.

Moving from Kline Street to Thirty-sixth Street, to a house with a bathroom. The First World War breaks up the family.

When we left 807 Kline Street—where my mother took me when I was a child, and Catherine was born there—Miss Gertrude Davis (this was the schoolteacher that wanted to adopt me and my mother wouldn't let her; I only wish to God she had, I would have been someone today), she moved. She built her own home, and Catherine's father, he built it for her. And when the home was furnished, we moved into the house that she moved out of on Thirty-sixth Street. Well, that was thirty dollars a month. Now, this is getting up in those days. This is where . . . would you say the better class lived, or the middle class? I don't know which one it was. But there was doctors and schoolteachers and professional people that lived around there.

And this is the first bathroom that we had. The bath was at the head of the steps on the left. And straight ahead was "Granddad's" room—that was Miss Gertrude and Miss Alma's father. And there was three bedrooms up there.

I enjoyed lighting the light in the hall. It was a chain hanging down, and you would pull this chain, and as the lamp came down to you, you would light it in this beautiful light in the hallway. And the living room had—everybody used velvet draperies in those days—the living room had sliding doors, and when you wanted to close off the dining room, there were sliding doors; I loved those doors. And then there was a room that led out of the dining room into the hall. There was a big, big porch that was enclosed. You had to pass through that porch to get to the kitchen; the kitchen was not joined onto the rest of the house, so therefore you never knew what was cooking in the kitchen because the kitchen was off by itself, see? And we often ate on the porch. That was the most beautiful house that we lived in.

But the war started. The First World War. And Mr. Henry—John Henry Ashe, Catherine's father—he had to go in the service. My mother couldn't pay that rent. There was no way in the world for her to pay that rent and take care of two children. Well, he went, he went into the service, and my mother used to write him every day and send him a package of everything she could get her hands on. He smoked cigarettes. She would send him warm socks and everything.

*Wartime economies: using Aunt Jemima sacks
for clothes, curtains, bedspreads, pillowcases
and dishcloths.*

Oh, there's so many things that come back to me. So many
things about the First World War. You could only buy five
cents' worth of sugar. And the sugar and everything came in
sacks. The grits and the rice came in sacks. They were white.
Aunt Jemima sacks. Because all of my little drawers and my
little slips had Aunt Jemima right on my backside. My mother
would take them and bleach them in lye, and boil them—
she'd boil the clothes, then spread them out in the sun. And
finally Aunt Jemima kinda faded away. Our pillowcases were
made out of those sacks, but beautiful hand-crocheted, she
did, and beautiful embroidery. Even the spread on the bed
was made out of those sacks, but they were so gorgeous with
the embroidery work that was put into it, you wouldn't know
it was a sack. And where they were sewed together, that was
a beautiful stitch that she would take on them. The same thing
with the curtains. Even the dishcloths were made out of sacks.
And she only paid, I think it was five cents a sack—but the
man used to save them for her. Oh, she was brilliant. She was
brilliant.

1918 ✳︎✧✳︎ Savannah

*Erma watches one last Dixieland jazz funeral
procession.*

I remember something else. When I was a girl and they had
a funeral—you know, we didn't live far from the Ogeechee
Road—everybody that was anybody, it all depends on how
much you paid for your funeral, you had a band, you had an
orchestra. And, I would say, forty people or a fifty-piece band.
And on the way to cemetery—where we lived you could hear
the music before it got to the street, to Kline Street or Thirty-
sixth Street—they played "Nearer My God to Thee," "When
the Saints Go Marching In" and all these sad songs. And this
coffin, this hearse—it wasn't like the ones they have now—
you could see clean through and see the coffin in there. It
was jet-black, and it was pulled by horses. And the family
would be next to this hearse. You know, the flowers would
be next, and then the family. And hundreds of people from
all over—everybody left their homes. People on both sides of
the street would follow that band to the cemetery. Those days
they didn't do like they do now. They fixed the grave, shaped
the grave and everything. They used to let the bodies down

on some kind of straps—not like they have now, everything is automatic: you push a button and it goes down.

But they used to let them down with these straps. And when that body was down and they covered that grave, you didn't move, you stayed there until that grave was covered and shaped. And then the flowers was put on the grave, which was beautiful. It was really beautiful. And the family and the hearse would drive off.

And I am here to tell you that on the way back from that cemetery you never heard such Dixieland jazz music before in your life. They played the jazz—all kinds of jazz, just like they did in New Orleans. From the cemetery until when they got to the Union Station. And you talk— They danced! *I* was in it. My sister and I would be right out there in it, until one Sunday my mother came home unexpected, and she saw us.

She got off of the trolley car. She ran us down and caught us. I said, "Uh-oh, we're gonna get killed tonight. We're gonna get murdered tonight." She says, "What right do you have dancing and rejoicing and cutting up like this on Sunday?"

I said, "Well, all of the children, Mother, everybody does it, all of the children, oh, everybody—"

"Not you. Not *my* children. Have you done this before?"

Now, don't lie to my mother. Don't lie to my mother, because if you lie to her, she'd kill you.

I said, "Yes, ma'am."

"When?"

I says, "Every time they have a funeral, we do it."

"So—every Sunday."

Those days, funerals, all funerals, had to be on Sundays. I don't know why.

So she says, "All right. It's now three-thirty, isn't it?"

I said, "Yes, ma'am."

She says, "You and Catherine go on and take your bath and put on your gowns."

I said, "Well, we have to make the ice cream."

"Oh, we're gonna have ice cream," she says, "but you're not gonna help make it. Go to bed."

I said to Catherine, "What is she gonna do now?"

"Well, why don't you ask her?"

"Who? The warden? You remember those men with the chains around their legs—that's what she'll do to us next."

So I went out and I asked her, "Momma, what are you gonna do? You're putting us to bed and you say you're gonna make the ice cream. You can't make it by yourself."

"I'm not gonna make it by myself. I'm getting the children down the street to come in and help me. And I have a cake that I baked on the job. And we're gonna have ice cream and cake."

Ohhh!

I ran back. I said, "Catherine, we can go to bed. We're being punished just by going to bed."

So Momma said, "Oh no you're not. Oh no you're not." She said, "At four o'clock, at five o'clock, you're getting out of that bed and you're gonna eat your dinner, and you're going back to bed."

I said, "Well, what about the ice cream and cake?"

"No. No ice cream and cake."

Well, I cried—that's the first time in my life that I cried to get a licking: "Momma, please. Momma, give me a spanking. Momma, please don't. Momma, please."

And we almost died, to hear them churn the ice cream churn. And we could hear the children say, "Ooooh! Look at that pretty cake." She used to decorate the cakes, you know. "Ooooh! Look at that cake." And we almost died in that room. You're talking about serving a prison sentence? That's what we did. That's what we did—punishment! Oh, if she had whipped us, given us a licking or something, it wouldn't have been as bad as this. But the warden knew what she was doing.

* * *

We never followed another band. The saints went marching home by themselves, because we didn't follow them. That's right. Never! When we heard the music coming, we stayed home. We didn't even go to the corner, to Ogeechee Road, which wasn't about a quarter of a block. But we didn't go. We stayed home. *That* was enough for us right there.

*Officer Coldstark and the judge in a woman's
dress intervene on Erma's behalf.*

I remember when I was a little girl about seven years old. As
I told you, my mother always told us, "Never take candy from
a man. Never get in a car or a truck or any kind of vehicle
or buggy or hack with a man. If a man said anything to you,
keep on going."

Well now, they used to have what you called watchmen
when they were building these large buildings, because the
boys would go in there and take the wood and take it home
and burn it for fuel. So they was building a place on West
Broad Street, and they had this man there—I would say he
was about sixty years old. He was the watchman.

We used to wear, the days when we went skating, black
bloomers and a white middy blouse like the sailors used to
wear with the big collar in the back, and you had a black tie
that came around that. This is what we wore when we went
skating. Oh, you *had* to have on that—you wouldn't be found
dead skating without your middy blouse and your bloomers.

Well, one of my wheels came off and I'm sitting there

on the curb trying to fix it and trying to find the little piece that came out of it.

So this man said to me, "What are you doing?" Old white man about sixty.

I said, "My skate came off."

He said, "Oh, I can fix that for you. Come on with me, I'll fix it for you."

I forgot what my mother told me, and I went with him. And when we got to the door, he said, "You'll have to come downstairs."

I said, "Well, what kind of a place is that down here?"

He said, "This is the basement."

I said, "I've never seen a basement before."

He had a lantern burning down there—he had two.

And I went on down there with him, and he took a nail—I took the other skate off—and he took a nail and put it through this skate and banged it.

He said, "This will last you until you can get it fixed."

"Ohh!" I said. "Thank you, mister, thank you so much."

So he said, "Now, before I give you your skate, there's something you have to do."

I said, "What do I have to do, what do you mean?"

He says, "I want you to take your pants down. Take your panties down and I want to look."

"What do you want to look for? Look at what? There's nothing down there to look for."

He says, "Well, I want to look."

And all of a sudden it hit me: This is danger; this is what my mother's been telling me. And up those stairs I went two or three at a time, and I didn't stop running until I got home. And by the time I got home I was screaming—scared to death. I knew it was something wrong, it was danger. What it was, I didn't know. And I knew that was what she had been telling me all the time.

When she could get me calmed down, I told her what happened.

She said, "Now you stay right here. Stay right here until I come back."

Well, we had a police. Those days the policemens rode the horses. They didn't carry pistols. They had a stick—they called it the billy. So she went and got Coldstark, who we all loved. We loved him, because he saw that you went to school. You didn't play hooky around that neighborhood. And if you was brought back—picked up and brought back—by Coldstark from not going to school, you was disgraced, and it took you two or three months to live it down. So she came with him.

He on the horse, and her and I in this hack. So the man was sitting outside on a box by the door.

So Coldstark went over to him, he says, "Do you know this child? Have you seen this little girl before?"

He said, "Seen what? I've never seen that little nigger before." He says, "I don't bother these niggers around here."

Coldstark says, "Don't call her a nigger. She's a little girl. She's a child. And don't you call her a nigger." He says, "You look more like a nigger than she does, because you're a grown man and you should know better. Now, don't call her a nigger—okay?"

He said, "What . . . what are you asking me all these questions?"

Coldstark said, "Did you take her down in your basement?"

The man said, "No. I never saw this little . . . oh, this little girl before."

I says, "All I want is my skates. You give me my skates."

He said, "I don't know who she's talking about. She doesn't know who she's talking about. She's never been here before."

So Coldstark said, "Let's go down in the basement." We went down in the basement.

I said, "There are my skates! There are my skates!"

My mother said, "Those are her skates, because I painted

them myself." She had painted the wheels silver, like the paint that you put on a radiator or something.

And Coldstark said, "Those are her skates, all right, because I've seen her use them. I've seen her with them so many times."

So he brought the man on upstairs and he took him to a box. They had these red boxes, like for a fire—they were painted red. And called up, and the paddy wagon came—that's what they called it. It looked like a hearse to me. It had a step on the back, and it had two places on the back that you could hold on to. Now, the policemens didn't get in there with the prisoners. The prisoners was put in, and they locked the gate, the doors to the outside, and the police stood on this platform, this step, and held on to these two rods.

Well now, I never saw the man any more. But I know two days after that they took me to this building. I had never seen a man with a woman's dress on—that's what *I* thought it was. And this man came up with beautiful gray hair, and he had on this black— Well, now I know it was a robe, but I thought it was a dress.

And I said to him, "Well, I never saw a man with a woman's dress on before."

And my mother says, "That is not a dress, Erma. It's a robe."

"Well, why do you have to wear that? Wouldn't you rather have on trousers? Pants? You'd look better than with that dress on—that looks awful."

He says, "All judges have to wear this, little girl. What is your name"

I said, "Erma."

He said, "Now, Erma, what happened when you lost—when your skate's wheel came off? Will you tell me? Just you and I go to talking. We don't want your mother or Coldstark."

I said, "If you send Coldstark away, I will not tell you anything."

"Why?"

I said, "Because I love him, and he would not let you hurt me."

He said, "I'm not going to hurt you. I'm here to protect you, to keep you from getting hurt."

So my mother says, "Now, Erma, Coldstark and I are going outside. He's not going to hurt you. You tell the judge the truth."

And I *told* him.

So he gave me a sucker.

I said, "I'm sorry, I can't take that."

"Why not?"

"Well, my mother said that we weren't supposed to take anything from a man or a boy."

"All right, Erma." He says, "Now, when your mother comes in, if I get her permission, can you take it?"

I said, "Uh—yes, sir."

So he called them in, and he said, "Can she have a sucker? Can I give her this piece of candy?"

My mother said, "Of course. Yes."

I said, "But you told me that I couldn't—"

She said, "This is different, Erma. But nobody else, do you understand?"

I said, "Yes, ma'am."

So I took it.

I said, "Well, I have a sister. Can I have one for her?"

He said, "Of course you can." He says, "I'll tell you what I'm going to do. I'm going to give you this whole bag of suckers, and your mother can give them to you as she wants. Is that all right with you?"

"Ohhh, yes!"

*Economizing with Aunt Ida in Yamacraw slum.
Erma's mother and Aunt Ida clash. Being
put out by Aunt Ida, and taken in by Pearl
Jones.*

Well, then when my mother couldn't keep her house, she
and my Aunt Ida got a house together, and my mother didn't
want to go. Because it was known as very bad—rough kind
of people lived down there. They didn't care, they would take
your head off in a minute. The name of the place was Yamacraw. And to this day I'm glad that they tore it down; and
the projects are there now. I wouldn't be found dead down
there *now*. But I don't know what happened to those bad
people—they're not there any more. Those people aren't there
any more; I guess they've moved away or died out or something.

And where my mother and my aunt lived, it had three
big bedrooms upstairs and another room where Catherine and
I slept. It really was a kitchen, but it was so big—the kitchen
was on one side and my mother had draperies across the room,
and that's where Catherine and I slept in that bed there, off
of the kitchen. And everything in there was blue and white.
The houses were all gay on the inside.

And we had a great big table. Well, most of the furniture

in the house was really my mother's. My Aunt Ida didn't have much furniture—matter of fact, she didn't have any. I think she had a bedroom suite, and that was all.

I have never seen my mother with a man. I have never seen my mother take a drink. She smoked a pipe. I have never heard my mother use a bad word.

So when Aunt Ida moved in with her, I remember her telling her, "Ida, I have two girls, and I want them to be brought up like we were brought up. Do you understand what I'm talking about?"

Aunt Ida said yes.

Well, I didn't know what my mother meant. But I found out later that my Aunt Ida was a little different from my mother.

And we were happy there, we lived together there very happy, until one day I came home from school and there was this man there with my aunt. I had never seen anything like that before in my life what I saw that day. And I didn't stop running until I got to the Oglethorpe Club; I was out of breath and I could hardly talk. And I was telling my mother . . . well, I thought the man was beating my aunt. I thought, I said, he's, well, he was, you know, he was beating her, and I said she can't even get up because he's on the top of her and he's beating her. And my mother brought me home, and she told my aunt, she said, "You will have to move, because I told you before you came here that I had two daughters. You will have to move."

You know, my mother was taken sick that night; she never got out of that bed.

When she got sick, we didn't know anything about cancer those days. What did people know about cancer? Well, anyway, she began to lose weight. I was eight then, going on nine; I was promoted to second grade but I never had a chance to go back because I was taking care of her. (You know, I've been taking care of sick people all of my life. That's the truth.) And she kept losing weight, and losing weight, and, well, everybody said—those days they used to call it consumption; they didn't say TB or tuberculosis—it was consumption, Laura has consumption. Nobody came near. Nobody. All those people that she had fed—nobody came. And poor little me, I was so little, I'd wash the sheets and things and put them on the line. And the bed, her bed, was even with the window. And she'd see. And I cried because I was so little, trying to get them on the line—by the time I'd get the prop up, the end of the sheets would be dirty. So she said to me one day—well, Savannah's sandy—she says, "Baby, put the prop up and pour the water—throw some water and it'll come off." And I did. I threw this water, and all of the sand and everything came off. So that's how I used to wash the sheets.

And before anybody ever showed me how to make a bed in a hospital and change a patient in a bed, I knew how, because I did it with her. I'd bathe her and roll her over. And the first time I saw cancer in my life I was nine years old. I knew exactly what it looked like. Because she had it from here all the way down. It was a great big red rose turned wrong side. But I took care of her, but I didn't know what it was.

You know, God moves in a mysterious way and He performs wonders to behold, and you better believe it, you better believe it. Just as the Bible says, bread upon the water will come back to you. It's true—

I remember my mother being so sick, and I had never seen snow. This was on a Saturday. This man came, put my mother in a rocking chair and had another man to help him take her downstairs, and sat her on the sidewalk. And her bed and the little bed that my sister and I slept in. "Oh, my

48

God—where are we going? Aunt Ida, what are we gonna do? You putting us out?"

"Yes," she said, "your mother have TBs, have consumption, and I can't catch it. And you children sleep in there with her—you have to go."

"Well, where are we going?"

"I don't know, but you can't stay here."

My Aunt Ida put her out on the street, furniture and all, and this woman—Miss Pearl—that's the woman that I left with. Well, anyway, put her out in the street and Miss Pearl took her in because my mother fed her—she had been feeding her for years the food that she would bring from the club. But she charged her rent—she had to pay rent, which was three dollars a week. And I used to scrub—go around and scrub these stoops. It's a porch, you know, but they call them stoops. And you used to have to use lye, and I would have sores on my hand from scrubbing these porches, but I made enough to pay that three dollars a week rent and for us to eat off. So I have been working ever since I was nine years old. I have been working all of my life.

And that's where my poor mother ended up, in one of Miss Pearl's rooms. There were large steps to get up to the rooms. And the stove and all the furniture—packed outside in a little house in the yard.

*Mother sings, and Erma takes piano and violin
    lessons.*

When my mother lived, I did take piano lessons, and violin.
I was about nine years old.

I could not tell you one word of music today. I couldn't
carry a note; as they say down *here,* I couldn't *tote* a note in
a *bucket.* So that leaves me out with music.

But I still love to sing, because my mother did, and that's
just *in* me. You're *born* with it. It's *there.* You're born with it.

I couldn't carry a note if it was as big as this house.

My mother had the most beautiful voice in the world, I think.
And she could play anything that anyone . . . any kind of
music, but she didn't know a note if it was brought to her and
if it was the size of a house. She didn't know anything about
music. But yet, she played it. And sang so beautifully. As a
matter of fact, everyone in the family sang—all my whole
family.

And she was determined that I would play. And that's
why I love it.

So I started. She started me off with piano lessons, and

violin. That only lasted a year, because after she got sick there was no more.

I visited my music teacher. She also taught violin. She was a great big fat black woman that used a long pencil to crack you on your fingers or your knuckles when you made a mistake. Her name was Mrs. Eloise Holmes. Eloise Holmes. Oh, yes. And I was doing just wonderful until my mother died. I had finished the first grade, promoted to the second, and I had learned how to pick up little tunes.

When my mother was living, I was taking music lessons, violin lessons, but after she died, that was it. It was all over.

And I forgot—there's so much I have forgotten about the music. I know the scales and the lines—E,G,B,D,F—and the spaces—F,A,C,E—and that's it. And the violin—I wouldn't do it, touch a violin! Because I know everybody would faint if I did. But to hear someone play a violin today—I mean really *play* on a violin, really *play* it—it breaks my heart, and I go to pieces. I cry. I'm not crying because the music is sad. I'm crying because the music is so beautiful. It really is, it's so gorgeous.

And, like opera—I do the same thing with opera. Now, the language that they sing in, I don't understand it. Most operas are sung in Italian. But I go, I cry with it. I don't know—God gives me the sense to know *what's* going on, *what* they're saying.

*Erma's mother dies at thirty-two. Erma picks a
gold coffin and has a mystic experience.*

In about two weeks time she was really a skeleton. And she
sent for her brother. He came. And I remember her saying to
him in the hospital, "Angus, whatever you do, never let
Allen have Erma. Never. Promise me that." "What about
Catherine?" "Don't worry about Catherine. She will always
be able to take care of herself. But not Erma. You promise me
that. That's all I want, and I can die in peace."

My uncle took me to Allendale, South Carolina, where
I was born. But I hadn't been back, see. I'd been back when
I buried my sister, my oldest sister, but I was a child. And I
stayed there with him for I guess about a month. He had just
started to enroll me in school.

And we had a baby grand piano with the legs cut off,
under the house. The house was rather tall. And he told me,
he said, "Your mother used to play that piano all the time."
And that's where, every day, I was playing that piano.

They had this old-fashioned hearse, the great big old huge
thing, the angels painted all over it, and oh, you could see the

coffin from the inside—oh, it was horrible. And the horses pulled it. They had two great big black horses that pulled this hearse. And my sister and cousins and I, we always went with them to see who was the ugliest. The people used to make the most horrible faces. I said, "Well, look at that one there, look at that one." But when my mother died—and I used to hear my Uncle Angus say, "Boy, business is kinda bad, it's kinda slow"—when my mother died, I didn't know anything about it. I didn't know she was dead. But he said to me, "Erma," he says, "anyone that you loved more than anyone in the whole world, which one of these coffins would you pick?" I said, "This one." The bronze had just come out. And to me it was gold, see. It was beautiful. And he kept asking, and I kept saying, "This one." So my uncle, this was Viola's father, said, "You've asked the child fifteen times. She keeps saying that one, so . . ." Angus said, "That's the most important, most expensive." "That's all right, I'll go fifty-fifty."

I didn't know . . . I didn't have the slightest idea that I was picking out my mother's coffin. I didn't know. So there was an undertaker in Savannah and I'm quite sure he's still there—Monroe, undertaker—he took care of everything. My uncle furnished the coffin and the box.

And everybody stayed home from school that day. All the children was all dressed. And I was under the house playing "Coonshine Baby."

Now, that undertaker—you couldn't keep me out of there. Because if anyone came in there—if it was a man, I put lipstick on it; if it was a baby, I took it out and played with it. You couldn't keep me out of there. But this day I was underneath the house playing "Coonshine Baby." All the children played it:

"De-dá dá-da dá dá dá
De-dé dé-de dá dá dá."

You played it. Two fingers. Playing "Coonshine Baby." And here comes the most beautiful white lamb I ever seen in my life. And you know how a baby lamb goes *baaaaaaa.* And he came over, sat right on the top of the piano. So I stopped playing and I looked at him. Well, look at this beautiful baby lamb. And when I touched him, it just disappeared. Well, that's the funniest thing I've ever seen in my life. So I started playing "Coonshine Baby" again.

And here come this great big beautiful snow-white lamb. Oh, he was gorgeous. But this time he was a little larger. He came over and I touched him. He disappeared. I stopped. I was petrified. I knew something was wrong. I said I've heard the children talking about ghosts and spirits and things, and I've been in that undertaker's so many times that I know something is wrong. This isn't right.

I was so scared, I started to scream—and out from under that house I had business. I ran inside. Everybody was standing there. There were about seventy-five people in there, but I didn't even know them. And an old lady by the name of Mrs.—I think her name was Cactus, she was related to us, she was white. She says, "Don't cry, darling, the Lord giveth and the Lord taketh away. Blessed be the name of the Lord." And I don't know what she's talking about. What was she talking about?

By that time the train was coming, slowing down and blowing. You always knew when there was a body on the train—it blew different. I said, "Oh, there's a body on the train. They got a body on the train. There's a coffin on the train. There's a coffin on the train." And I heard her say to Aunt Lye—that was my uncle's wife—"Doesn't she know?" She said, "Erma, come here. What was you crying about when you came in here?" And I told them about the lamb. "What lamb?" And I explained it. Nobody said a word. "You actually . . ." I said, "Yes, that lamb came the second time. I knew that lamb was not real, and it frightened me." By that

time the train had began to move on, and when it moved—
then I knew that my mother was dead. But I didn't know what
was in store for me. I didn't know the hell that I would have
to go through. But I found out—oh, my God, I found out.

Erma learns her father is not in heaven. She meets him; he beats her; she beats him. She runs away for the first time.

Now, as far as my father is concerned, I didn't know anything about him. We lived right there in Savannah and I didn't know anything about him. She always told me that he was in heaven, so I presumed, well, my father was dead.

After my mother died, my uncle came and he took me home. Uncle Angus—he's the one that had the undertaker. And oh, in about three weeks—I was going to go to school and everything—here comes my father. Well, I had to go with my father; he was my father. I didn't want to go—I tried to die, but anyhow, I had to go.

And when we got there, got to Savannah, I met this woman that I had been hearing my uncle talk about, Ella, and how my father left and all. I said I thought he was dead, I thought he was in heaven. My uncle says, "No, he's in Savannah, and he's coming for you." I said, "I'm not going." He says, "Oh, you'll have to go." I said, "I'm not going." But I had to go. So, uh, my uncle was going to go to court, but said, "Well, what's the sense, there's nothing I can do. He's her father."

So, anyway, I went with my father. I got my little butt torn up that same day. I had never been stripped before in my life. My mother would spank us—oh, on our legs or on our little butt. But he made me take off all my clothes and beat me because I wouldn't call this woman Momma. I couldn't call her Momma. I didn't know nothing about the woman. You can't beat a child, make a child love you. You have to earn that child's love, you have to get the . . . you know. And I still never called her Momma; I called her Miss Ella.

Well, I caught hell with him and her. There wasn't a day that went by that they weren't on me. If he didn't beat me, she did. I didn't know what it was to sit to the table to eat; I ate out on the steps. She got a little pie pan from the five-and-ten, and that was my plate and I ate on the back steps. I couldn't go to the table to sit to eat.

And I knew a little bit about playing the piano—just a little bit. And they had a piano. And she came in and I was playing this piano, and she tried to kill me. I wasn't allowed to touch it. I couldn't touch the piano, I couldn't play the piano. And he wasn't man enough to say . . . well, leave her alone, she's a child and she's been studying music. He said, "You know, maybe I'll see that you go back and take up with your music lessons, Erma." She says, "No, you won't. I'm not wasting any money on her." No music lessons, that was out. He wasn't a man, he wasn't a man at all.

That was the meanest woman I ever saw. Ohhh, my God, that was the meanest woman I ever saw in my life. She told me—there I am, I was about nine years old then—she told me one day, "I want you to cook some rice." There's a lot of grown women right now can't cook dry rice—it's gooey. I said, "Well, I don't know how to cook the rice." She said, "You go out there and you cook four cups of rice." Four cups of rice—that's an awful lot of rice, you know. I says, "How much water should I put in?" She says, "Cook the rice."

Well, my father had a garbage can. I went out there and I cooked this rice, and it was just like hominy grits. She made me dump it in this can. Four more cups. And by the time my father came home, that thing was . . . about like this with rice.

Now, he didn't believe in beating you with your clothes on, you had to get buck-naked. You had to strip. Well, I had never been stripped before—I didn't know what that was to be stripped, to be beaten. I don't mean like you would whip a child, I mean beaten like you would an animal.

So she says to him, "Allen, I want to show you what Erma did. She's playin cookin."

"I'm playin cookin?" I said. "I wasn't playin cookin," I says. "You told me—"

"Are you calling me a liar?" Bam! she hit me.

She beat me every time that rice came out bad. And he beat me. That went on for about—oh, I guess, about two months, about two months.

So one day he came home, and he had been drinking. And she told him that I had messed up. What was it I messed up this time? Something she had told me to cook and I couldn't get it right, I couldn't cook it. Macaroni and cheese. Well, all she had to do was to tell me or show me, you know. There was this great big dish of macaroni and cheese that I had messed up.

Well, she had beat me all day. *He's gonna kill me, I know he's gonna kill me.* They used to have these big bolsters on the bed—not the pillows, the big bolsters. And they used to have the doorstops that was made out of bricks—they would cover them with velvet. So he went out and I saw it—I was looking out the window—he got this bottle, drinking out of it. *Oh, God, he's gonna kill me. He's gonna kill me today.* I got that brick, put it underneath that bolster.

He came in and he said to me, he said, "I want— Take your clothes off."

I said, "I'm not takin my clothes off."

He said, "Well, I'm not going to . . . I can't, uh . . .

58

The flesh will heal up, but not the clothes. They'd have to be sewn. Take them off."

And then he would tie you like this, see, tie you up like that. What you gonna do? Nothing you can do. Where you going? When you're tied up by your hands, where you going? I said, "I'm not takin my clothes off, Daddy." He said, "You better have them off when I come back in here." He went outside again and I looked out the window—he got another drink. *Oh, God, he's gonna kill me.*

You know what I did? I got that brick from underneath the pillow, and got up on my knees in the bed, and when he came in there and he reached up here like this to snatch my clothes off, I took that brick and brought it right down here.

I grew up right then. I grew up right *then* . . . when he reached up to grab me by the collar to tear my clothes off, and I just took that brick from under that pillow and jumped up, stood up, and brought it down over his head. I hit him twice, and the blood was everywhere. Out the window I had business, out the window.

And I went to this woman, this Pearl. This was the woman that my mother had been so good to. I went to her. And she says, "Erma," she says, "you know, I'm leaving to go to Florida, tomorrow." She said, "I'll take you with me. You're big enough to work."

I should have stayed with my father.

Life with Mrs. Pearl Jones during the Florida land boom. A lot of work, but little to eat and a sack to sleep on. The moonshine / bootleg business.

I liked Miss Pearl about as much as I liked any of my mother's friends, but she and my mother were much closer, you know. That's why when I got in trouble, when I ran away from my father, that's why I went to Miss Pearl.

And when they got ready to leave, and went to go in business for themselves, everybody was shocked. No one thought that she, that they, had enough money to go and open a restaurant, but that's what she told them that she was gonna do.

And when I went there, the day before they left there, when my father came there looking for me, I was under the bed.

She says, "No, I haven't seen her."

So she said to me, "You're big enough to work. You been working for your father."

I said, "I'll do anything." I said, "I can work."

So she . . . her husband said, "Let's take her."

So they did. So they left that next day. I didn't have on shoes. I didn't know what a pair of shoes was any more. They took me barefoot on the train. We left there that Sunday, that Sunday evening, with the one little dress that I had on.

Her sister lived in the country, so I never got a chance to see Jacksonville. Her sister lived in the country, and we stayed there, I think, a week or so. And the lady that later on delivered my son was her cousin. She lived in West Palm Beach, Florida. She had found this restaurant for Miss Pearl, and the house, which was right next door to her.

And we went on to West Palm Beach.

Monday, I saw the woman looking through the papers. Do you know, she got me a job. Eight dollars a week, taking care of a beautiful little red-head boy with the prettiest blue eyes I've ever seen in my life. Stayed there, and just like I got my money, that's the way I had to bring it home.

Well, she found out that that wasn't enough money— and West Palm Beach Laundry, she got me a job working there. And I was so small—the place, you know, where they dry the rugs (they called it a tumbler then; I don't know what they call it now), the rugs and the big thick heavy pieces—they built me a little platform. And I used to work, I used to do that. And that was fifteen dollars a week, and just the way that I got that fifteen dollars a week in a little brown envelope, that's the way I had to take it home to her.

Miss Pearl fixed the house up, got some furniture and put it in there, rented out the two bedrooms—all you had to do was put up a sign that said "Room for Rent" and it was taken, it was gone! Because those days they were building up West Palm Beach. There was so much construction work going on. This was about, oh, 1923—no, about 1922.

And she catered to the workingmen. Now, they had a

restaurant. Well, I worked there, I worked there in the restaurant, but I had to sleep behind the counter because she had the other rooms rented out. And I didn't know what it was to sleep in a bed. You know where I slept? Behind the counter, on croker sacks. When you have worked from three o'clock in the morning until you're ready to drop dead on your feet, you'll sleep anywhere.

And on Thursdays, it was a kinda dull day, I did the laundry. Now, those days in the laundry you had what they call a bench that a carpenter would make for you, and you had four tin tubs on that bench. You had a pot—you see a lot of these pots down here with the three legs, these big iron pots; I have one here right in my yard—and mostly that's what they used to boil their clothes in. They didn't have Clorox. These tubs would set up—each leg would set up on a brick, high enough that you could get the wood under there. Well, you wouldn't fill it all the way to the top, because you had to put the clothes in.

Now, the clothes . . . You would put in your lye—they used lye; my mother used to use Red Devil lye, I remember that, and so did Miss Pearl. And they'd use this Red Devil lye and put that in the water. And the powder that they used, it was called Gold Dust Twins, and those days—I see they're using it now; it came out again—Oxydol. But my mother always used the Gold Dust Twins. It was in an orange kind of box with two little black children on it. That I will never forget. And they had soap—it was called Octagon soap. It was a yellow soap; it came in bars, big bars for laundry.

Now, the washboards were made. They had certain carpenters to make the washboards. It was made out of wood, which was much better than the tin boards, and they last for years. They really did, they last for years.

You wash the clothes. Each garment was washed by hand on that board. They were taken to the boiler pot, and they were boiled for about half an hour in this powder and this lye, which had dissolved by then. The water was boiling when you put the clothes in there. And those clothes boiled.

You had a stick, something like a broomstick handle or an ax handle, something like that you kept for that purpose. And you would take that stick and go over there with the tub and put the clothes on that stick—pick it up, each piece—and put it in that tub, and take it back to where the washboard was. But this time you have clean water in there.

Now, remember now, all of this water has to be carried from the hydrant, the spigot—or whatever name they call it down there—bucket by bucket (they didn't say "pail," they said "bucket") to fill up these four tubs of water that was on this water bench.

In the water that you had washed the clothes in the first time, while the white clothes are boiling, you'd wash out the other, colored clothes. And after the colored clothes were washed up, then you got the dustcloths and things like that, you know.

And then, when you threw that water out and put clean water in there, you put a little more soap powder—not too much. You use your soap, your Octagon soap, and you scrubbed those clothes *all over again*. They were put in, then they were rinsed out—they were put in the other tub of water. And then they were rinsed out of that tub and put in another tub of water. Then they were rinsed out of *that* tub—all this is done by hand—and put in the last rinse, which was called the *bluing* water. The bluing came in liquid and it came in a powder form, with the little wrap, the little pieces of cloth. My mother liked the liquids the best, that's what she used, and Miss Pearl liked it too, she used that also.

And when you got through with those clothes . . . You boiled everything—everything was boiled but the ladies' . . . you know, if you had something silk. Even the cotton dresses, the men's dungarees, the men's work shirts—everything was boiled. And when you got through taking the things out of the bluing water and putting them on the line, they were as white as the dripping snow. Even the *dust*cloths were boiled. They were as white as the dripping snow. The sheets and all of the clothes were hung on the line. But the dustcloths and the rags and things, they were spread on the grass. And they were just *beautiful.* They weren't *dingy* like the clothes we have now. Because the things, what we have now, this Clorox—I don't know. I think I'm going to start boiling mine—my husband's T-shirts and things like that—because they don't look *white* to me. I told him that the other day. He laughed at me. He said, "What are you going to do, start cooking my clothes?"

So I did the clothes on Thursdays, and then I would go back and start on the dishes that was left over from lunch. If they wouldn't do them, I'd have to get there and do them and get ready for supper.

And as far as loving Miss Pearl—now, I never loved her. I was afraid of her. When I went to live with her, I was deathly afraid of her. I thought I was afraid of my father, but I was deathly afraid of her. She chopped me on my finger with the butcher knife. Another time she struck me with a piece of wood. I was . . . I don't think there was anyone in the world that I was more afraid of than I was that woman. Many days I cried, I said I should have stayed with my father.

She was arrested several times. Because those days there was no such a thing as whiskey, you know. There were no such a thing as liquor stores. But now I didn't know what was going on. I didn't know. She never let me see anything. I guess she was afraid that I would say something about it to somebody. But I know they arrested her, and I couldn't understand. What did they arrest her for? She didn't do anything. I didn't have any sense. I didn't know what they arrested her for. So about four months after that they arrested her again. They took her—both of them. And I was there; she hired another girl to help me run the restaurant. So I said to her, "Why do they keep arresting her? She don't bother anybody, she doesn't, she hasn't done anything." She said, "I don't know." But she knew. She knew I was stupid and didn't know any better. Miss Pearl was selling moonshine. That's what she was doing.

Erma, eleven years old, is healed with the help of spiderwebs. She is advised to run away again and to get married, which she does.

Then I was about eleven years old—just about eleven. I wasn't allowed to eat anything out of there but black-eyed peas or beans, and rice. And I don't eat black-eyed peas today or *any* kind. And I remember I have taken scraps off of the plates that people would leave, and eat it. I've even gone in the garbage—when we'd rake the food in the garbage, I would steal stuff out of there and eat it. I had to.

That lady . . . I was cleaning some fish one day, and I didn't cut the fish just right. Now, a fish sandwich was only ten cents those days. That's when Miss Pearl took the butcher knife and chopped me across my finger. And there was another lady, Miss Alice, there. She said, "Oh, my God. Oh, my God." She said, "How could you do that to that child?" Well, that finger, it never straightened out right. Well, it wouldn't heal up, so this same woman, she says, "I tell you what you do. You come around to my house and I'll fix it for you." She got some sugar, some yellow Octagon soap and spiderwebs, and put it on this finger and bandaged it up. It healed it. That might sound stupid, but it really healed it. And she says to me, "Why don't you get married?" Well, there was no such thing those days as getting an annulment; when you were married, that was it.

I said, "I don't know anybody to marry." I didn't know anything about boys. I never had a chance to talk to a boy.

So there was a fellow that roomed with her. He was from the Bahamas. He said, "You know, it's a shame." So one day he came in there, the restaurant, to buy something, and he dropped his change—I think it was fifty cents. It rolled around, and he came behind the counter to try to find it, and there I was on these croker sacks. So he went back and he told Miss Alice, he said, "It's a shame before God. That child sleeps there on the croker sacks."

He said, "Is this where you sleep?"

I said, "Yes. Yes, sir."

He said, "Don't you go home?"

I said, "No, sir."

So Miss Alice, when I went back around there the next time, she says, "Erma, run away."

I said, "I did that once before, and they got me, they found me."

She said, "If you could just get married, they couldn't do anything with you. Because once you're married, you're married."

And he says, "Do you know something? I'll marry you."

I said, "You *will?*"

He said, "Yes, I'll marry you."

So we got married. But this is the way we got married— we had the minister to come to the house and marry us. We didn't have any license or anything. We didn't get that until we went to Philadelphia to get married again, see. We left there and we went to . . . As a matter of fact, he sent me to his sister, and when he came to see me, he said, "You know, I don't think I'm going back." Because Mr. Deese offered him a job right there. This was Indian River, the name of the orange grove.

*The "most beautiful days of my life" in a cottage
under the oaks, picking oranges, cutting
bananas, drying fish and raising chickens.*

To go back to Florida—I loved it there. I think those were
the most beautiful days of my life. We used to pick oranges.
The man picked the oranges. My husband drived the truck.
And while he was driving the truck—you know, to take the
oranges to the warehouse—I would what you call "ground
the trees," which means that you pick out the thickest oranges,
the thickest row, and I would get all of the oranges off of the
bottom as low as I could, and when he came back he would
get the top. So therefore, we made hundreds of dollars a week.
Well, the ladies, they all put up a fuss—they didn't like it
because my husband was making more money than they were.
It wasn't my fault that they had a house full of children. And
what made it so bad, I was the only American woman there.
They were all from the Bahamas; they called them "Nassaus"
—"Nassaus" or West Indians—which I ended up marrying
one of them. And we had this little three-room house. And
those were the happiest days of my life that I can think about.
We did not have electricity. We had a little stove that burned
wood and coal. And we had no heat, but you didn't need heat

in those days—you do now—in Florida. And we raised our own vegetables, and I've always canned, put up everything that I use all of my life. I still do. And I've always had my garden.

Where our home was—it was under these gorgeous trees, the most beautiful oak trees you've ever seen in your life. Here was this little cottage sitting under all these gorgeous oaks, but we weren't the only ones that was there. I sat every morning inside of the house. The house was screened, the porch was screened—I mean, screened completely, so a fly couldn't get in. And I would watch all of these different snakes, early in the morning when it was cool, crawling across the ground. Because it was so hot down there, you very seldom saw a snake when it was hot.

It was years later when I had chickens. I had about three thousand head of chickens, and when I came North, before the bottom fell out of the banks, you know, and everybody was going bankrupt, Erma went and got her money out of the bank. And I hid it underneath the house in a Mason jar. And it took me three weeks to get my money from underneath that house because there was a bunch of snakes that made up their mind that that was going to be their home. And what could I do? I didn't want my husband to know that I had the money, because he was the type that money comes, money goes. Well, I waited and I waited, and finally they went away and I dug up my Mason jar and I got my money and I said to him, "We're going to New York."

He said, "What are we going on? Nobody has no money?"

Who had money in the bank, it was all gone. But I had mine—I wasn't worried, the snakes was on the top of it.

But before we leave Florida, we worked at a place called the Blue Goose Orange Company. And the Indian River Orange Company. And that Indian River separated us from Long

Island. You go over to Long Island, and I used to get in a *bateau*—that's a little old boat with two oars—and cross that five-mile river. I *would*. I never knew how to swim, I don't know how. I wasn't afraid. And come back loaded down—well, the grapes just hung over the river; they were wild grapes—loaded down with grapes. And they had a long, huge knife that the Mexicans use—I can't remember the name—the machete. I can't remember the name of this huge knife, but it was sharp as a razor. Cut down one bunch at a time of bananas—the whole thing, see, you brought back home. And the mangoes were like the hair on your head. Get four or five bushels of those, brought that back. I used to do this, I used to do it. And there was a fruit that we called guava—you made jelly out of it. And the coconuts. I didn't like the green coconuts, but the men seemed to like them. But the mangoes by the bushels.

It was all so beautiful. It was in Bonaventure, Florida, not far from Cocoa, Florida. The name of the oranges were Indian . . . Indian River, I think—and Blue Goose. And across the street, I mean across the *river*, the river that separated us from Long Island—the name of the river was Banana River. And I would get in that boat and row across there—just me—and didn't think anything about it, and couldn't swim a lick. But I would do it.

Of course, I didn't know what a dress was. I wore pants all the time—dungarees. *Not* dungarees—those days you wore overalls, the ones that comes up with the bib. I see they're coming back in style. Now, can you imagine me in this place that was infested with rattlesnakes, and I was never bitten. So you see, I had a guardian angel watching over me.

It was beautiful. Things was *beautiful*.

And, like, fish. The men would go out with their nets, and they would catch enough fish . . . They had a fish down there, I've never seen it up here—I think they called it the *jack* fish. The flesh was dark, and we smoked it. What wasn't

71

smoked was hung up to dry, was salted and hung up to dry in the sun.

And those days the ladies down there, they knew nothing about canning. Everything was dried. The okra was cut and dried in the sun, and it didn't take but two days to do it. As a matter of fact, you could do it in one day—that's how *hot* it was. The okra was spread out on a clean sheet, and four to six people would go and take the sheets at the corners and in the center and shake it up and let it go back down again. And I'll tell you, by night it was like rocks. And when you got ready to use the okra, you only soaked it overnight and it was just as pretty and green, as fresh as it was just cut.

The same with the fish. The fish was salted and peppered, and hung on the line to dry. Now, you put it out about three days—you took it in each night because it was always a heavy dew—and in three days that fish was as hard as a rock. When you got ready to use that fish, it was soaked overnight also. But as a matter of fact, you changed the water two to three times, because I never liked too much salt. And it was delicious—much better than the fresh fish. I wished I had a piece right now—that's right.

And when the men *really* went fishing, when the fish was really biting, they would come back with truckloads of fish. And it all depends on how many children you had, how large your family was, depends on the amount that was left. And I have cleaned four and five—ten—tubs of fish at one time. That's right.

We never had venison there, and I don't know today why, but we never had venison. But any other kind of game we had. And don't say anything about a *rattlesnake* steak. Now, the blacks wouldn't eat it. You couldn't find a black person that would touch a piece of rattlesnake steak, because they were afraid of it. *I* wouldn't. If it was cooked . . . I had some friends, friends of mine, some white friends, that bought these gorgeous steaks—and they were beautiful. The meat looked so pretty. I had a brand-new frying pan. Do you know, I threw it away after they left. No, indeed—scared to death of the poison.

But now, the frog legs—we loved them—we had those quite a bit.

Erma, twelve years old, gives birth to a son.

Well, after I ran away from Miss Pearl and got married and moved away from there, her cousin told me why she was being arrested. I said, "I didn't know anything about it. I never saw it." She said, "Of course you didn't see it." And this cousin of hers told her where I was living. That's how she happened to find me. And this cousin of hers, she was what you called a midwife. She was the one that delivered my baby.

I didn't even know I was pregnant. What did I know about being pregnant? Most women stop, you know, seeing monthly what they see monthly, and I didn't. I never did stop. But one day I was sitting on a porch, and she kept looking at me. She said, "Come here and let me look in your eyes." I said, "Look in my *eyes?*" She said, "Yes, come here." And I wasn't any larger—I hadn't gotten any larger. She looked in my eyes, she said, "Uh-oh." I says, "What?" She says, "I see another pair of eyes there." I said, "What are you talking about?" She says, "You're pregnant." I said to myself, This woman must be crazy—how can she look in my eyes and say that I'm pregnant? I says, "Well, I'm not either." She says, "Oh yes you are." I says, "Well, how could I be pregnant?" She says, "You're doing the same thing any other married woman would do. That's how you're pregnant." I said, "No I'm not." She said, "Oh yes you are."

So she told my husband, "You better take her to the doctor." And he took me to the doctor. He says, "Well, good God, you don't know you're pregnant? You're in your fifth month." And I hadn't . . . I was the same size I always had been. And I didn't get any larger until about the seventh month. It looked like it happened overnight. The bust was the only thing that really was growing; the other part, it didn't start until I was in my seventh month.

And then, having this baby—you're talking about going through hell. I didn't go to no hospital. I went to see the doctor once, and he said yes, that I was pregnant; I didn't go back to the doctor. Those days you didn't do that. You had no kind of treatments or anything.

And the baby, the baby, my baby—I was four days and four nights in labor. I could have died, which I learned later that I should have died then; but I don't know why—God wanted me here for some purpose. And this old lady—she's sitting up there drinking her moonshine, and I'm . . . I felt like I was climbing the wall. And every time I would scream, she would tell me to shut up. She said to me, "You didn't scream when you was getting that baby."

So I said to her—I'm gonna show you how stupid I was— "Well, aren't you gonna cut my stomach open?" She said, "Cut the stomach open? For what?" I says, "To take the baby. How am I . . . To take the baby." She says, "The baby's going just how he went in there." I said, "Well, how did he get in there?" She says, "Well, of all the stupid." She said, "You are stupid. You're stupid. You'll find out how he got in there."

I'd scream every once in a while, and she'd come over there and look at me, touch me, feel my stomach, and go back and sit down and take another drink. And for four days and four nights I almost died. And when the baby was finally born, in the last minute they had to call a doctor. And he cut me. And the poor baby! The baby's head had been there so long until when it came out—when he cut me, the baby came out, see—the little head had been there so long it was the most hideous thing you ever saw. It had swollen, the top of the head had swollen. It was the ugliest thing that you ever saw in your life, and I turned away, I didn't want to see it. I didn't—ohhh, I never saw anything like that!—I didn't want to see it.

Mrs. Pearl Jones reappears for a quick visit and kidnaps Erma's baby, James. Erma's husband tires of searching.

I told you about my son. When he was three months old the lady that I lived with—she and her husband—came to visit my husband and I. We were living in Bonaventure, Florida, then, at the time. Mrs. Pearl Jones and James Jones. They came and they said they was going to stay three or four days with us. Well, I wasn't particular about having them, because I never cared anything for the woman, you know, on account of the way she treated me. But my husband, he says, "Well, let bygones be bygones." So when she says she was gonna stay three or four days, I said to myself, Well, my God, where will we sleep? We'll have to sleep on the floor—because we only had three little rooms.

Well, they stayed two days, and she couldn't keep her hands off of my baby. And I told her, I says, "You know, now I have to take in washing"—this is what I was doing then, taking in washing—I says, "and I cannot take care of the baby if you're gonna spoil him. I have him trained so he just lie there and sleep, and when he's not sleeping, he's playing, he's sucking his thumb." I had him on a quilt on the floor. So I don't like the idea of holding him so much, but she did.

So we were talking about frog legs. My husband and I started talking about the dairy—we used to go out and get the frog legs. And she said she'd never had them. I said, "Well, they're beautiful, they're larger than chicken legs are." Well, she certainly would like to have some. "Well," I said, "it's about two hours—about an hour drive there, an hour drive back—so it'd be about two hours." She says, "Well, why don't you and Jack go over and I'll stay here and take care of the baby." And her husband said yes. I said, "Well, don't *you* want to go?" He says, "No, I'm gonna fix my tires. They don't look so good to me. Look like they're gettin a little flat." We went and left them there with the baby.

And when we came back, the car was gone, the baby was gone. So we didn't pay it any mind because we figured, well, they're riding around and she took the baby with her. So about two hours after, I got a little uneasy. I said to him, "I don't like this. Let's ride around and see if we can find them." I don't know whether you remember the old Fords that Henry Ford put out, these high-topped things that you could sit in the back. If it rained, God bless you. A rumble seat, I think they called them. Well, anyway, this is what we had. Tin Lizzie—we called it a Tin Lizzie. And we went all over, and we couldn't find that woman. I didn't find that woman till fourteen years later. We looked all over, we went from one place to another, as little money as we could get together and save up, and we would hear about, think that she was there, we would go there. We went to Savannah four times; we couldn't find her.

They had no police there. They had the sheriff and his deputies. No, they didn't care anything about a black child being lost. He said, "No, he'll turn up. The lady just took him for a ride somewhere. He'll turn up." So the next day I went back to him, I said, "We haven't seen him." He said, "Well, so what do you want *me* to do about it?" Those days, if you were born black, you were cursed the day you was born. So every time someone would write and tell me that they'd seen her in Savannah, we'd take off, in the Tin Lizzie.

What did I feel like, being without my baby? I thought I would lose my mind. I thought I would go crazy. You would say, "Well, a child your age, you're nothing but a child—what do you know about a baby?" Oh, you know. You know—a young animal that has a baby will try and protect it. That's why I can't understand how mothers can give their children away or put them up for adoption or leave them, and put them in garbage cans or things like that.

I'll tell you what I did one day. I was so desperate. I saw a baby in a carriage, and something said to me, Take the baby, take that baby and go with it. And I started to think—stopped, and I said to myself, Well, what should I . . . why would I do that? And put that mother through what I have been through? She would go through the same hell that I'm going through. Oh, I felt so ashamed of myself. How could I ever think of doing a thing like that! No, no way.

And when my husband . . . No, he wasn't as interested as I was—he was only interested in one thing the whole time we were married, and that was women. That was all—women. He took me to Savannah four times, and the last time he said, "This is it. If he's around the corner, he can stay there." Well, I tried to die. But I think I kept hoping and praying that I would see him, that I would find him, until I think about ten years, and I thought, Well, I know I'll never see him any more. This is it. I will never see him any more. He's gone. I will never see my son any more. And I never had any more children—thank God. Thank God.

*Erma, sixteen years old, is successful in the chicken
and egg business before the Depression hits
Florida. She and her husband survive a
terrible hurricane.*

Someone gave me five hens and a rooster, and from those five
hens and a rooster, then I think I bought ten more hens and
I began to raise chickens. And the chickens . . . well, we
never bought groceries. My eggs and fryers paid off all of my
grocery bills—besides money to put away, which my husband
knew nothing about.

Before the Depression started, we had this terrible, *terrible* hurricane down there. And we—my husband and I—was
tied up in a tree. He knew, because he was from the Bahamas
and he knew about these things. I didn't. We were in the
house. He said to me, "Let's go." He went up the tree, tied
me, tied the rope around me, and up the tree he had business.
And I had never climbed a tree before; well, he climbed it like
a monkey would climb a tree. He pulled me up. And we saw
our home, our little Tin Lizzie, our chickens—and everything that we owned—go, like a piece of paper. And what
really broke my heart, it was a baby was on a door. The mother
and father must have put this child on this door to try to save

it. And I was hysterical because I couldn't get down and get that *baby*. But he wouldn't let me go. I would have been dead, of course; I would have drowned. When the hurricane—when the storm—was over, the ships was in the cemetery. You could not see the top of a house. Everything was under water. It was horrible.

But *I* had gone to the bank—I had accumulated ten thousand dollars, off of eggs and chickens furnished to hotels and restaurants. Nobody knew anything about this but God and I, see. Before the storm broke I went to the bank and asked for my money. They said I couldn't get it all at one time. "What do you mean I can't get it all at one time?" I'm a dreamer. I'm really a dreamer—I still am. Anything that comes to me in my dream, you may as well look out for it because it's going to happen. Well, I dreamed that I was supposed to go and get my money out of the bank. I went. They wouldn't give it all to me. They said you can only get about five thousand. "When can I get the other?" In two weeks time. I took it home. I told you first I hid it under the house with the snakes. Then I sewed it inside of a pillow, and I slept on it every night. The second week I went back and I got the other five thousand. I took the money. I made a belt and put it around my waist, then put my girdle on. And my husband did not know one thing that I had, about the money.

When the hurricane was all over, no one had anything to eat or any place to go. I knew where I was going—as far away from Florida as I could go. And I can't remember what year that was, but it was one of the worst years that I've ever seen in my life. I remember going to the kitchens; you know, the soup kitchens feeding the people hot soup. And when all of the food was fed, when all of the whites were fed, they put water in it and it was slop, and they would give it to the blacks. And I couldn't eat; I couldn't eat. I starved; I just couldn't eat. And then if you were eating and some little child looked at you with those great big hungry eyes, you still couldn't eat. So what you do, you give it to the children. My husband and I both did the same thing.

1928 ✳⌘✳ The Atlantic Coast Line Railroad

Erma and her husband take the train to New York City.

It was the Atlantic Coast Line. And when you went in the station, there was a chain that separated the blacks from the whites. Those days, there was no such thing as air conditioning; the windows were open. The baggage car was next to the engine; we were next to . . . the blacks were next to the baggage car. It was dirty, filthy, grime. When we got to New York, I was so dirty and filthy, my head was so filthy, the only thing I wanted to do was take a bath. And as far as going to the rest room, that was out of the question. I opened the door and closed it back.

There were people on there with children. And those days people had large families. And I didn't know—we didn't know—any better. We were told that they had a dining car on the train. I bought the tickets, to begin with, because my husband was from the Bahamas and he didn't speak very good English; so I bought the tickets. So about twelve-fifteen I said to him, "I'm hungry." He says, "Well, we'll ask the conductor when he comes back by where, how far do we have to walk down to get to the dining room." Because we were told that they served hot meals. And we weren't told that they were served for white only—we didn't know that. So I asked him, I said, "How far down do we have to go to get to the dining room?" He said, "Dining room?" I said, "Yes." He says, "Niggers don't go in the dining room. That's only for whites." I says, "What?" He says, "Niggers aren't allowed in the dining room—you bring your damn lunch on the train with you. Didn't you know that?" I says, "Have you ever been in the dining room?" He said, "Of course, I have my meals in the dining room." I said, "I thought you just said that niggers weren't allowed in there?" Well, he turned as red as a tomato. My husband says to me, "Will you shut up?"

So, those days, they had a drink out that was named Orange Crush, and sarsaparilla—I wish they had it today because the sarsaparilla was the best thing in the world you could use for gas. I loved it. Coca-Cola wasn't popular then; Orange Crush was the thing. And we drank Orange Crush, and there was a black man that came by with peanuts and little peanut-butter cookies and Fig Newtons and gingersnaps. That's the kind of junk we ate.

And the scenery—there wasn't any scenery. There was nothing beautiful at all. This train that we went on was a local, and that's exactly what it was. It was like a bus; it stopped at every, every little station, and you saw the little shanty houses by the tracks. Most were black—poor blacks. Some were poor whites. And the only thing that I really enjoyed seeing through the train, the windows, was the cotton and the peanuts and the cattle. But other than that, there was really nothing to see.

Now, we started from Savannah, Georgia. Then South Carolina and North Carolina. And we stopped in Atlanta and Richmond, Virginia, and Washington, D. C.—where we changed trains, and thank God, I could go to the rest room.

The train, the seats were horrible, they were hard, very uncomfortable, but *clean*. The rest room was clean, but we still couldn't go to get anything to eat. That was all right. Then Maryland, Philadelphia, Jersey, New York. And it was the Atlantic Coast Line.

Erma and her husband learn their first lesson about New York economics and are dazzled by the night lights.

Well, I remember the night that I arrived there. Now, when I got into New York, it was at night. When we got off the train, well, I was like Alice in Wonderland. Because I had never seen such a huge building before. That I remember.

I didn't ask anyone which way to go. I just followed the signs and finally ended up outside on the sidewalk. I had never seen such beautiful scenery in my life—all lit up. All of these *people*—all of these hundreds of thousands of people walking up and down the sidewalk. Well, my God!

And we stood there about ten minutes, waiting for a cab. All these cabs were passing and passing and passing, and I didn't see any black Checkers. That's what they had down in Savannah, because blacks didn't use the Yellow Cabs. They weren't allowed. These Yellow Cabs would come by and say, "Taxi, mister? Taxi? Taxi? Taxi?" Well, of course, we stood there waiting for some *black* cabdriver.

I stood there until I just got tired. So one man came over to me, a porter, a black porter.

He said, "Lady, do you want a cab?"

I said, "Yes, but I can't find any. Where could I get a cab? Nothing but the Yellow Cabs are passing."

He said, "Well, why don't you get in it? What difference does it make what *color* they are?"

I said, "Are you allowed to ride in the Yellow Cabs?"

He said, "Well, of course, lady." He says, "You're from the South, aren't you?"

I said, "Yes, I am."

"Oh, I see." He says, "Yes. You can ride in the Yellow Cabs. It doesn't make any difference," he says. "They don't look at your color. The only thing they're interested in up here is the money. They don't care what color you are. They look at that green and silver—that's all they want. They're out here to make a living."

Well, when we got in the cab I thanked him—and when we got in the cab, I didn't say anything to my husband and he didn't say anything to me, because we were both just struck by the beauty of the lights. It looked as if God had just taken the stars and sprinkled them all over the world—that's the way it looked to me that night. It was just beautiful.

The cabdriver drove us all over Broadway, and I was still like Alice in Wonderland. I wasn't watching the meter to see how much it was, which it would have only taken sixty or seventy cents from the station to my aunt's house. And he knew that we were country. He knew we were country. I told the driver where we were going, but he could look at us and see country *all over us*. By these little cheap cardboard bags that we had, and I guess the way we were dressed.

So I didn't mind the extra fare because I had never seen anything like this. Now, the buildings—I didn't see them that night. But the lights, up and down Broadway, and the people.

And then I noticed—I said to him, "Listen, you've been around here, you've taken us around this place about three times. What are you doing? Riding around in circles?"

My husband said, "Shut up!"

87

He says, "Oh, that's right. You want to go to 538 Lenox Avenue."

I said, "That's what I told you when I got into the cab."

"Oh!"

So he took us on to 538 Lenox Avenue, and when we got there, I said to myself, My God! I hope that my aunt is still here.

Erma locates Aunt Eliza in the high-rent district.

We got out, took our little bags, little cheap cardboard bags. And I looked at this great big huge house, this building. Although it was at night, you could look . . . you could see the lights, you know, all the way up. And I think she lived on the ninth floor. I said, "Well, this is an awful big house for her to own"—I didn't know anything about apartments.

So we went on in, and there was a man there in uniform. The lobby was just gorgeous, it was just gorgeous. He says, "Lady, who do you want to see." I said, "Miss Elizabeth Jones. Does she live here?" He said, "Oh, my God, Miss Jones has been living here for thirty-five or forty years." I said, "How far up does she live?" instead of saying "What floor?" I didn't know. I said, "How far up does she live?" He said, "On the ninth floor." So I says to my husband, "Let's go, let's walk." The man said, "Lady, you can't go up there." I said, "Why not? She's my aunt." He says, "You will have to be announced." "Well, what do you mean?" He said, "I will have to find out whether she wants to see you or not." So he went to this phone and he called up. I heard him say to her,

"Not this one. Your niece is here to see you." I heard him say, "Not this one." But I didn't know until later when she said she told him, "You don't know who my niece is, so why would you call to send her up?" But he'd never seen me before.

So I went up there and I knocked on the door. They had these little peepholes in the door. And a maid dressed in a black uniform with a little white apron and a tiny little cap sitting on her head opened the door. She said, "Yes?" I said, "I would like to see my aunt." She says, "Your aunt?" I said, "Yes." She says, "Honey, I don't think your aunt lives here." And she looked at us from our head to our feet—country, you know. I said, "Yes, she does." She said, "What's her name?" I said, "Elizabeth Jones." She said, "Well, you will just stay here a minute, just wait a minute." And she closed the door.

And when the door opened again, my aunt opened it. I said, "How are you, Aunt Eliza?" And she looked at me. Here was this gorgeous woman, this beautiful woman. She was more Indian than the rest of us. She always wore her hair in two big huge braids way down past her waistline. She said, "Which one of the brothers' or sisters' children are you?" She says, "I know you're a Best." I said, "I am Laura Best Milledge's child." She says, "Which one are you, Erma or Catherine?" I said, "I'm Erma." She says, "My God, come on in, darling." So we went in. She told the girl to get us something cool to drink. I said to her, "Do you know what I would like to do before I do anything else?" She said, "What?" I says, "Take a bath." I said, "I am *filthy*." My husband says, "I am too." She said, "Well, all right, Erma, you go and take a bath. Wash your hair." She was a beautician. She says, "You just wash your hair, and just tie it up and I'll have someone come in to do it for you." I didn't know she had a chain of beauty shops—I didn't know that. But the house was so gorgeous, it was just beautiful. The furniture and everything—I'd never seen anything like that before.

So I had told my husband before we got up there, "Don't say anything about any money." Because I was told that if you go to New York, they're gonna bleed you, they're gonna take everything you've got. "Don't mention money!" "All right." And I had my bath, and my husband he went and he had a bath, and God, I felt like a different person because I was filthy. I had my hair tied up in a towel. About, oh, in about half an hour this woman was over there and she did my hair for me. It was beautiful, because I'd never had my hair done like that. In those days it was at my shoulder; they used to wear the page. And I looked like a different person when she got through with my hair. So I said, "How did you get that lady to come over here?" She said, "She works for me." She said, "I have seven beauty shops here." Ohh.

She says, "Come on inside and sit down." I didn't want to go in there because her furniture—the slipcovers were all white, snow-white. I said, "I'd rather sit here." She says, "Come on in. You have changed your clothes. You can't soil anything. So what?" She said, "I'll have them cleaned again." I still didn't want to go in. I said, "I'll feel better sitting right here." "Erma," she says, "you're in New York now. Leave the country behind." So we went on in, and we sat there and we started talking.

And the first thing I said to her was, "Where is Aunt Ida?" Now, that's really who I wanted to see. That was the one that put my mother out, in the rain, in the wintertime, and it stayed with me all my life. All my life I wanted to tell just what I thought of her: one of these days I'll see her and I'll tell her. She says, "Ida lives with Effie." I said, "Where does Aunt Effie live?" She says, "In Brooklyn." "Oh, I see."

She says, "Well, Erma, where have you been all of this time?" I says, "In Florida." She says, "Well, why didn't you get in touch with some of us?" "Why should I? When Momma died," I said, "nobody showed up. We kept her body for four days waiting for her sisters and one brother; nobody showed up." I said, "You all knew where I was. Nobody cared, because nobody wanted the responsibility of raising a child." She didn't say anything, but she began to cry. So I said,

"Now, there's no use for that. I'm so glad to see you." I said, "You haven't changed. You still have that beautiful hair." But I didn't know her hair was dyed jet-black, because her hair was snow-white but I didn't know it. Because I didn't know anything about the hair being dyed those days.

So I asked her, I said, "Is there any place that we . . . do you have a place here that we could stay until I can find a place?" She said, "Yes," she says, "I have an extra little room." She says, "It's rather small." She said, "It will cost you twelve dollars a week." I said, "How much is it?" She said, "Twelve dollars a week." Well, I almost dropped dead, because that's what you paid a week down here for a *house*. Eight and twelve dollars. So I said, "Well, my goodness, rent's *high* here." She said, "Oh yes, rent is very high in New York." So she took us back to this little room. So help me God, it was a little room. You could sit on the bed and open the dresser drawer. It had one window in there, and one chair, and one dresser. And when you opened the window, there was nothing but bricks—the apartment next door. Just bricks. I felt like I was in *jail*. Because I wasn't used to being closed up like that.

*The streets of New York. Erma on her first
morning in the city ventures out.*

The next morning, I think about seven o'clock, I was downstairs, on the steps. And the first thing that hit me was the
sidewalks. I'd never seen such wide sidewalks. My goodness,
I thought, these sidewalks are as wide as some of the roads,
where I came from. And then I noticed how wide the streets
were.

And so many people, going up and down, like ants or a
bunch of bees. Backwards and forwards on both sides of the
street. The subway was right to the next corner.

I didn't get it. I knew they weren't going to work, because no one had on any work clothes. Everybody was dressed.
They were wealthy and dressed up to me, as far as I could see.
Because, you know, in the South they used to wear—they
don't do it now—but they used to wear cotton dresses, starched
cotton dresses, and the men wore overalls. Not dungarees—
overalls—and they were starched so stiff you could stand them
up on the floor. But all these people were dressed. I was won-
dering, Where in the world are they going?

I was standing there saying, "Good morning, good morning, good morning, good morning," like somebody crazy. And they turned around and looked at me. Some laughed and some just went on, and I guess said, Well, she's out of her head or something.

So then I was told that you don't say good morning, you don't speak to people, or good evening. You don't do that. Well, *that* shocked me. I never could get used to the people passing each other and not speaking. Well, I found out that they didn't even speak to the ones that lived in the buildings. Even in the elevator, no one said anything to you.

Erma takes her first subway ride. She learns how to get to Brooklyn, finds her Aunt Effie and Aunt Ida, and forgives Ida.

When my aunt took me for a ride on the subway I was, oh, like a child that had never been . . . well, you know how children are when they've never done anything or seen anything before. That's the way I was.

She took me downtown, and I couldn't talk. I couldn't say anything. She would say something to me. She would say, "Erma, do you hear what I'm saying?"

"Yes, ma'am. But I was trying to take in everything at one time."

But I said to her the next day, "I would like to go and see Aunt Effie."

She showed me the maps on the subway—you know, right by the door there's a map there. She says, "You can't go to Brooklyn by yourself, Erma."

I said, "Oh yes I can."

She says, "No you can't. You'll get lost."

I said, "If you tell me which train to take, just tell me which train to take and where to get off, I can go."

She says, "When you get out of the subway, Effie's house

is right in the front of the subway. You just walk across the street. It's right there: 1516 Fulton Street."

I said, "I can find it."

She said, "Well, take the phone number, in case you get lost."

I said, "All right."

She said, "Now, if you get lost in Brooklyn, here is Effie's phone number."

I said, "All right."

So I went. I wouldn't sit down. I stood right by the door, by that map, because I knew I had to get off at Hall Street.

She says, "You can't miss it, because it's a big department store. You'll see all these figures, these designs, clothes and everything in the window." She says, "You can't miss it."

And I stood there by that door. I guess people thought I was crazy, or nuts. Because I wouldn't sit, and that time of day there was plenty of seats.

When I got to Hall Street, I got up and walked up, went upstairs, crossed the street like she said, and there it was: 1516 Fulton Street. She had lived there for thirty-five, no, about forty years I imagine. About forty years.

And I rang the bell. No answer. Well, it wasn't like where my aunt lived, because where Aunt Eliza lived it was, well, a different class altogether. And this place you had to walk up the steps, and she lived on the fourth floor, and I had to walk up those flights of steps. My God! Well, anyway, I got up there and she said her apartment is—"Well, just knock on the door, because there's only one person on each floor." Okay, I did that.

Well, what I really wanted to see was my Aunt Ida. I wanted to tell her just what I thought of her. Because, as I told you before, she put my mother out, in the rain, in the wintertime. I wanted to tell her just what I thought of her.

So I knocked on the door. This woman came to the door.

I said, "Hi, Aunt Effie." I would know her from anywhere. She had more hair on her head than I've ever seen on any woman in my life. Always did. She could never wear a hat.

She says, "Who are you?"

I said, "I'm Laura's daughter."

She says, "Which one? Erma or Catherine?"

I said, "I'm Erma."

She says, "My God! Come in, sweetheart." And she hugged me and kissed me.

Only thing I wanted to know was where is Aunt Ida. Because Aunt Eliza told me that Ida lived with her.

So I went on in. She had what you called a "cold-water flat." They had to make their own heat, which I'd never seen anything like that. They had to make their own heat.

And there was two . . . three women there. One sitting in a rocking chair and the other two ladies sitting there.

So I said to her, "Well, where is Aunt Ida?"

When I said "Aunt Ida" this old lady sitting in the rocking chair held her head up. She looked at me.

And Aunt Effie said, "Well, Erma, how do you know me and you don't know Ida?" She says, "You don't know your own aunt?"

I said, "I know Aunt Eliza, I know you, but I don't see Aunt Ida here anywhere."

And the only thing I could think about . . . well, wait, all of my mother's sisters had a head full of hair, and this old lady that was sitting in the chair, her hair was silver and she had a head . . . and I said, "Is this Aunt Ida?"

She said, "That's Aunt Ida."

So Aunt Ida says, "Are you my niece?"

I said, "Yes, I am."

"Well, which one are . . . who's . . . which brother or sister's child are you?"

I said, "I'm Laura Best's daughter—Erma."

And I thought her eyes was gonna pop out of her head.

I said, "You know something? I came here to tell you just how dirty I thought you was, and just—"

Aunt Effie said, "Erma!"

I said, "Just let me finish talking—and just what I thought of you." I says, "But I don't have to do that because I can see that God has taken care of that part."

She weighed about eighty pounds. And she started to cry. And I just stood there for about, oh, a second, I think, and all of the meanness and the hate that I had in my heart for her all these years, it just melted away, and I went over to her and I put my arms around her.

And she says, "Laura has forgiven me, Erma, your mother has forgiven me. Please? Can you forgive me? Please forgive me."

I said, "I forgive you." I said, "Who am I to not forgive anyone if I want God to forgive *me* for my sins?"

So we started to talking, and I said, "You know something? They kept Momma's body for four days waiting for her three sisters and brother to come down, and nobody came. Not one of you came. You was living too high and mighty. You couldn't come to see your baby sister buried."

Aunt Effie says, "Well, when Angus wrote us and told us that Laura was sick, we each sent ten dollars a week. That was thirty dollars a week."

I says, "Sent it to whom?"

"Sent it to Ida."

"Sent it to Aunt Ida? Well, we didn't get a cent."

Aunt Ida shook her head yes.

"Well, what did you do with the money?"

"I came up here on the Ocean steamship."

Aunt Effie said, "Ida, how could you do a thing like that?"

I said, "Well, it doesn't matter. It really doesn't matter."

So I stayed there awhile—oh, about four or five hours. And my aunt got all upset in New York, and she called.

Aunt Effie says, "Yeah! She's been here for four hours."

Aunt Eliza said, "My God! You mean to tell me she found her way over there?"

She says, "Yes."

"So you think that we should come over and get her?"

She said, "I don't know. You better talk to her."

So she said, "Erma, we're coming—"

I said, "No, you're not, either. I came over here by myself and I'm coming back by myself." And I did. I did.

*Aunt Ida and Aunt Effie in the Gypsy section on
   Fulton Street. Erma smells incense and dreams
   a lucky number.*

I didn't have anyone to visit but Aunt Effie, and she lived in Brooklyn.

And where Aunt Effie lived over in Brooklyn, there was about four blocks of nothing but Gypsies. And they had these curtains, all kind of different beautiful color of satin material over the front. They lived in storefronts.

And the front is where the people used to go in there and have their fortune told. Not me. And they lived in the back.

And they had children like a hen laying eggs, as far as I could see.

You know, I always was afraid of Gypsies. I think I told you that they tried to steal Vinie once.

The shop that my aunts used to go in all the time, it was right downstairs from Aunt Ida, where she lived, Aunt Ida and Aunt Effie, because Aunt Ida was living with her then.

Now, it was one thing that they had in there that I really did like—that was incense. To use, you know, when you cooked fish and cabbage. Other than that, I don't understand that place today.

And that whole block, most of that block, there was nothing but Gypsies on both sides of the street, those days. That's where it was located.

This store—I still can't tell you what kind of a store that was, because it was not really a drugstore. They had all kind of salves in there, I don't know what they were used for. It was really more like a Gypsy store, I would say. And they had . . . oh, incense. They had what they called a Lucky Number incense. You would burn this incense. It came in little squares. You would burn this incense and a number would show up in the ashes. I remember that. But I never used it because I didn't play it, I wouldn't gamble on it unless I'd dream it. I'd give 'em hell *then*.

The store that I bought my aunt's medicine . . . This really makes me laugh because today I don't understand this store. That was a different kind of store. I've never seen any like it before or since. The only thing they had in there was candy, incense, a lot of junk. Aunt Effie *lived* in the store, and Aunt Eliza and Aunt Ida was just as bad. I saw no pills, no lipstick, no powder, no face powder for the ladies, no baby powder or anything, you know, that ladies could buy. They had a lot of incense and junk that I didn't know anything about. But they had a *lot* of Gypsies in there. They were buying too. I still don't understand it.

It was not a drugstore. It wasn't a drugstore. It was a store where they sold incense, candles and all kind of bright scarves—satin—and dream books of all kinds. The dream books—I remember those books because Aunt Eliza and Aunt Effie had them. As a matter of fact, all of the people in Harlem had them. There was *The Lucky Seven*. I can't remember the name of them all, but I remember *The Lucky Seven*.

They were for numbers. Because everybody, even the

pastor, everybody played the numbers. I did too. Because I could dream a number just like you would dream what tomorrow's gonna be. I never played a number unless I dreamed it. If I dreamed one, you may as well get your money ready because it's coming up. The largest amount of money I ever won on a number was $15,000 straight. And that number was 222. I dreamed that number on a Sunday. I told my Aunt Eliza, Aunt Effie, George Best—that's Rebecca's brother— and I think that was all. Oh yes, and I told my husband, Jack. We played the number that Monday. It didn't come out. So they got mad with me, because they knew every time I dreamed a number it comes out. They got mad with me, and they wouldn't play it any more. I played it that Tuesday, and I hit the jackpot. I certainly did. So Aunt Eliza she wanted me to give her . . . I think she wanted me to loan her five thousand dollars. I said, "I wouldn't loan you fifty cents." I wouldn't. Oh, we bought a car. And the rest of it, I put it in the bank.

Laura comes for Aunt Ida.

Before this aunt died, she didn't want anyone to give her her medicine, or touch her or come near her, but me. That's right. She died with her arms around me. I don't know what it is— I think God must have made me to take care of her. Oh, I stayed over there with her about three months. I told my husband, I says, "I have to go and help Aunt Effie, because Aunt Ida now is helpless, she's helpless as a baby." I says, "She can't control her bowels, and Aunt *Effie* is dying on her feet." So I went over there and stayed about three months. He would come over every night; he and Aunt Eliza would come over every night. Well, he had a very good job. He had to go back.

So she . . . when she died, she was a tiny little thing. You could pick her up in your arms. She died with the most beautiful smile on her face, but she scared the *hell* out of me one day, the Sunday that she died.

She told me that Saturday, she said, "Laura—where is Laura? You see Laura?"

I said, "No, she's in the kitchen." Well, there was a friend of hers by the name of Laura.

She said, "She's not in the kitchen. She's standing right there. You don't see your mother, Erma?"

I says, "No, ma'am."

She says, "Well, she has her arms around you."

Well, I think every hair stood up on the top of my head. If I had had on a wig, it would have stood up. I didn't *feel* anything.

I says, "Where is she?"

She says, "She has her arm around you and she's happy, she's smiling so beautiful." She says, "She came for me. She told me she was coming for me."

I said, "She did?"

She said, "Yes."

I said, "When is she coming for you? Is she here for you now? Huh!"

She says, "No, she'll be here for me at twelve o'clock. And it's not twelve o'clock."

This was on a Saturday.

So I went *out*. And I told Aunt Effie and my Uncle Carroll—we used to call him Uncle Pony; his name is Carroll Best—what had happened.

She says, "Well, she said that Laura had forgiven her. Maybe Laura *will* come for her. Maybe Laura will come for her."

I said, "How can she come for her? She's *dead*!"

"Erma," she says, "there's a lot of things that we don't understand. There's a lot of things that we don't understand."

I asked her how does Aunt Ida know that Laura had forgiven her. She said that Momma had told her that she'd forgiven her.

I said, "Now, this I don't understand. I don't understand any of this."

So the next day, which was Sunday, it was the most beautiful day! The same woman, Miss Laura, was there. They must have known that she was getting lower, you know. But I didn't know it.

Aunt Ida said, "Erma . . ."

I said, "Yes, ma'am?"

She says, "Will you get into bed with me?"

Well, I didn't want to get in the bed with her because she was wearing diapers and everything. I didn't want to get in the bed with her.

I said, "Aunt Ida, I don't want to get in the bed. It's too hot. I don't want to get in the bed."

She says, "Please."

I said, "Aunt Ida, I don't want to get in the bed."

She said, "Will you braid my hair?"

Well, she had loooong hair. I braided this hair all over.

And she said to my Aunt Effie, "Don't you dare take the braids out of my hair. She braided my hair and I want it to stay. Don't you dare take them out."

She said, "I'm not going to take them out, Ida!"

So I got in the bed, and I stayed along the top of the cover. I wouldn't get under the cover. And, you know, she couldn't move unless you moved her. She was nothing but a human skeleton. She had cancer. Aunt Ida had cancer. She had been a beautiful woman, a beautiful woman. And she had gone down from this beautiful woman to a woman that weighed eighty pounds.

The church bells would ring at twelve o'clock. And the church bells were ringing so beautiful. They did in those days. I don't know whether they still do in New York and Philadelphia and Brooklyn. But the church bells rang on Sunday—beautiful church songs they played.

And this beautiful church bell was ringing and it was such a gorgeous day—exactly twelve o'clock.

And *she turned over.* Now, we couldn't move her before. This is what I couldn't understand. She turned over, put her arms around my neck and just looked at me with the most beautiful smile that I've ever seen on anybody in my life. And she died with that smile on her face. And everybody kept saying, "Well, what a beautiful corpse!"

And just looked at me and just . . . *Ahh, ahhhhh.*

I said, "Well, thank God, she's gone to sleep."

So I stayed there about ten, fifteen minutes, and one of the ladies came in. She said, "Erma?"

I said, "Yes?" I said, "Shhhhhhhh. She's sleeping."

So she went out. So she came back again.

She said, "Erma?"

I said, "Yes?"

She said, "Why don't you get up?"

I said, "I don't want to wake her up." I said, "She's sleeping. This is the first time that she went to sleep without them giving her those pills. So why don't you just let her sleep."

So she went outside, and I heard my aunt scream. Both of my aunts screaming, and my uncle also crying.

I wonder what's happening out there.

So *she* went out and told them—I found out later. She said, "Ida's dead." And she said, "Erma thinks she's sleeping."

So my aunts didn't come in, or my uncle—but the lady, the same lady, came back.

She said, "Erma?"

I said, "Yes, ma'am?"

She moved my aunt's arm from around my neck. She says, "Get up."

I said, "I don't want to wake her."

She said, "You won't wake her. But get up now. You want her to be comfortable? Now you get up."

So I got up.

She said, "Erma?"

I said, "Yes, ma'am?"

After I got up, she says, "Your aunt is dead."

I says, "No she isn't."

She says, "Oh yes she is." She says, "She's dead, Erma.

She died exactly twelve o'clock. She said that Laura was coming for her at twelve o'clock, and that's when she died."

And my aunts, they came in and they were screaming and crying and my uncle was crying and carrying on, and they covered her face up.

I snatched the cover off. They called the doctor. He said she was dead. And as fast as they would cover her face I snatched the cover off. I didn't believe it. I wouldn't accept it. Because no one died like that. I thought you had to struggle or make some sound or something—not die that easy like that. And *smile!* This! I had never seen anything like this.

But there was a woman that weighed about a hundred and forty or sixty pounds, and didn't weigh no more than about eighty pounds when she died. So I wouldn't accept it until that evening when the undertaker began . . . when he took her. And I sat by her bed, right there, because they couldn't cover her face. I sat right there by her bed. And when the undertaker came and took her away I went to the window and saw them when they put her in this . . . it's not a hearse, it's the wagon they come to pick you up in. Then I realized that she was really dead, and then I went. I cried. I cried to break my heart. I did. We had grown very close in three months. She tried to make up for the things that she had done to my mother. And she tried to show me that she loved me. And we were very close.

So when it was time for her, they took her and brought her back to Allendale. I don't know which grave is my mother's and which was Aunt Ida's. Well, those are the two graves. The two sisters are there.

I couldn't go. I was sick. I was on the verge of a nervous breakdown. I couldn't go. Maybe it's a good thing I didn't go, because I guess I would have died.

So they came on back home. And my aunt had left— Those days ladies had beautiful dinner rings, they called them, they were rather long-like—and she had several of those. And she told Aunt Effie that she wanted me to have them, because Aunt Effie had all of her insurance. Aunt Eliza never did anything for her, so she left everything to Aunt Effie, and the jewelry to me.

So Aunt Effie says—

I said, "Well, I don't think it's fair for me to have all of her rings. I think Aunt Elizabeth—"

She said, "Elizabeth don't need any rings." She said, "I don't want them because I don't use them. I don't care for jewelry. So they're yours."

So we left the rings there, but when they came back from Allendale from burying my aunt, the rings were gone!

Aunt Effie's son had . . . he pawned them. He took and he pawned them. But he didn't pawn them in New York. We looked all over, we couldn't find them. So that was that. But it didn't matter to me, though. What did I care about diamonds, about jewelry, in those days? I still don't care much for them.

And—I don't know—there's so many memories that I have that I don't even like to talk about. That was one of them—when my aunt died.

Erma, being married to an older man, stays close to home.

I didn't like New York. I lived there, I think, eight years if I'm not mistaken, and I don't know any more about it than you do. Because I never went anywhere.

I wasn't able to do any shopping. My husband bought every stitch of clothes I wore. He did all the shopping. You know, those days, when the man was the head of the house, you didn't say anything. Of course, I didn't have any sense then. I was young and stupid and didn't know any better. And the store that he went shopping was right downstairs.

And about *going* anyplace. Huh! I couldn't. Because I knew I didn't have the right kind of clothes to wear, because my husband bought things for me like a woman forty years old.

The only fun that I really had up there was going window shopping. I loved that.

One place I used to go and look in so much, the lady would come to the door and say to me, "Why don't you come on in?" She would ask me if I wanted a job.

Look at all these beautiful clothes, and go home and put on those clothes for somebody forty or fifty years old!

I never did go anyplace. I never did go. Because, as I said, I married an older man, and he didn't want me to go anywhere, so I didn't go.

There was a lady upstairs. I would sneak up and talk to her, until Aunt Eliza found out about it. And she just let me know that this was not the South. So that was out.

The lady that lived upstairs—this lady that lived upstairs—she looked exactly like Aunt Jemima. So help me! What was her name? Tillman. Tillman. Her name was Miss Tillman.

She had good money, you better believe it. She used to go out to very wealthy women and do their hair. She made her own hair conditioner for their hair and their scalp—cream for that. She made cleansing cream. She made her own soap.

Nothing for blacks. Only the filthy wealthy whites. And she went to *their* homes. She did their hair.

And the lady, the girl next door, in the next apartment— she was from the South. I couldn't let my aunt see me talking to her, because she would kill me. She didn't like it up there, because she was a little country girl, you know, just like me.

The girl that was engaged to marry George—Katherine— my aunt told her and I not to open the front door, not unless you looked at that peephole, and to always put the chain on the door. There was the one time she didn't do it. She opened the door. She was raped and all that in that apartment.

Erma sees Bessie Smith in the neighborhood, at the Cotton Club.

The Cotton Club was not far from where we lived, on Lenox Avenue.

About going to look at the ladies at the Club. I used to sneak away. Oh, I did that about four or five times—when my husband would go to work. He'd come home after twelve from his job.

About Bessie Smith. Oh yes, I saw her. As the people would come up in their limousines—in these fine cars—the doorman would say, "Miss Bessie Smith," or "Miss Ethel Waters," and the people would applaud. I stood right there by the door to watch them.

Those days the ladies wore . . . everybody's hair was cut, everybody wore bobbed hair. There was no long hair hanging anywhere; everybody's hair was cut. And they wore stockings the color of your dress. Your stockings, your dress and your shoes were the same color. They called them "flappers" in those days. The shoes were real high, they were called spike-heel shoes, which was a very good thing to have because it makes a very good weapon to defend yourself with.

Because the heel—it's about three inches and the end of it was real keen. You could work on somebody's head with that. A lot of women used them for protection.

And she had on a white beaded gown. Well, those days the dresses were just at the knee—just above the knee, just a tiny bit above the knee. And this was a beaded gown, and the bags, most of the bags were beaded. And they would wear wide hats. Now, the stockings that the ladies wore those days, they weren't sheer. They were something like, I would say, glove silk. They used to have material that ladies used those days. And the stockings were fourteen and fifteen dollars a pair, if you could afford it, but they'd last you two or three years. They didn't get runs in them; the only way they could wear out was the heel would go first, or the toe. And as I said, the material . . . you didn't see the skin. Oh boy, those were the days. Those were the days.

There was one friend I had, that was Katherine. She was a chorus girl at the Cotton Club. And she was the one that got me the tickets to go in, and got me a dress and a pair of shoes, which my husband made me give them back. That young lady—I don't know her last name, her first name was Katherine. Rebecca's brother, George Best, was living with my Aunt Elizabeth. He had a room there. And this young lady was his girlfriend. I told you what happened to her.

Well, she would stop by the room, you know, to see her boyfriend when she wanted to. So she started staying there because it was nearer her job. You know, that was better than going all the way back to Jersey. That's where she came from, some little country place in Jersey—wasn't no Newark or anyplace like that; I know it was someplace from the country in Jersey. And that's where, that's how, I met Katherine.

She was the one that got me into the Cotton Club. I didn't have anything decent to wear to no place like that or anyplace else, because my husband dressed me like I was old. So she fixed my hair for me and loaned me this dress of hers and a pair of shoes. That's where I got the shoes. And that's the way I got to go into the Cotton Club.

And about the people that I saw going to the Cotton Club. That was Noble Sissle, I think his name was, Lionel Hampton, Duke Ellington! Ethel Waters with her "Stormy Weather." Peg Leg Bates! Cab Calloway. And Bingo Bill Robinson—he used to play with Shirley Temple. But I only saw them from the outside.

I loved to watch the ladies and their fine minks and diamonds, these beautiful women, the chauffeur-driven cars. Most black women with white men, because most all of them had a mistress up there in Harlem, which they still do.

And inside of the theater, it was just gorgeous, it was beautiful. The Cotton Club—it was just beautiful. The chairs were all velvet, soft. And as I said, people came from all over to go to this . . . to come to this place. Now, it cost an awful lot to get in there. But, I told you, I got in for nothing because the girl, one of the chorus girls that worked there, on the stage, she gave me a ticket. And the girls were beautiful, the chorus girls were just beautiful. They were gorgeous. They were all the same height, and all brown-skinned and *up*. You couldn't get in there . . . the chorus girls, you couldn't get a job if you were black, if your complexion was jet-black. That was it, you was out. Things have really changed now, though.

Friends of Aunt Eliza and white men.

In the North, about white men in the North—ever since the slaves have been brought over to this country, *that* has been going on. That's right.

I have been in some of the most beautiful homes, apartments—the most gorgeous apartments—friends of my Aunt Eliza. And I said to her, "How can they live like that?" Just gorgeous—interior decorating and all of that crap, you know. And they had rich white men that was keeping them. These men were married, but they always had a black mistress.

Erma has a last chance to see her dying father.

Well, you see, the thing about it was, I was on my own, because when my mother died, those people wasn't going to
take us. The whole family's educated, every one of them but
my sister and I. They had their parents to take care of them,
to do for them. We didn't have anyone.

And what I had for a father—that wasn't a father, that
was a pappy. I wouldn't even call him *that*. I knew when
he . . . he didn't see me. I think I was about twenty-one
years old when I heard that he was dying. Someone found
me accidentally and told me that he was dying and that he
wanted to see me. He was begging: If I could just walk up
to the door. You know, I wouldn't go! I wouldn't go.

My aunt said, "If you don't go, I'm through with you."

I said, "Well, you're just through with me. I'm not
going." I said, "If you had somebody strip you buck-naked
and beat you with a whip that you whip a horse with until
you bled, you wouldn't go either."

She says, "What?"

I said, "That's what he has done to me. Stripped me

buck-naked and hung me up by my two hands like you would a side of meat, and beat me with the whip that he used to use on the horse."

In time I might have forgiven him stripping me naked to beat me. But not his hands feeling me, feeling me. I tried to kill him then. I wasn't going to go to him now.

Aunt Eliza's health fails. She loses her business, fortune and friends.

We stayed there. We paid her by the week. When it was time for her to pay her rent, she didn't have a cent. *We* would have to pay the rent. So that went on and went on until I just got sick of it.

Now, she had a beauty shop. She got sick. She lost her business, and we stayed on there with her. We paid the bills. And I kept begging her, "Why don't you get out of this place and get something less expensive." My husband got a job right away. I said get something less expensive. It's too much money. I said we can't afford it.

Well, she cut her toe with the razor blade. And it got so bad they had to take her to the hospital. When she got to the hospital—now she's just about broke—she didn't want to go in the ward. She wanted a private room. I said, "Well, do you have insurance to cover it?" She said, "No." I said, "Well, you'll have to go in a ward, because I can't pay it and pay all of this rent. I just can't do it, and the electric bill and all, I can't do it."

She said, "Well, you have enough money."

I said, "I *had* enough money. Well, I don't have much now."

So anyway, they had to keep her in the hospital because gangrene had set in. Anyway, they took the toe off.

And while she was in the hospital, Aunt Effie found me an apartment—in Brooklyn. And we moved to Brooklyn, took all of the furniture and moved to Brooklyn. It was much cheaper. It was a nice place.

And when we went to bring her home—I didn't say anything to her about what we did—she tried to die: What will her friends say?

I said, "Aunt Eliza, you don't have any money. You spent up all your money." I said, "What you should do, some of the diamonds that you have, and that mink coat you have—you should sell it and help us, because I'm just about broke."

Oh no, she wasn't going to part with those things.

So I kept her there for about two years. I couldn't go anywhere. She was like an invalid. Meanwhile, this foot had broken out again. Had to take her back to the hospital, and it wouldn't heal up, and she wouldn't sign the papers for them to take the foot off.

So I went to see her one day, and they had her on the porch and it was freezing cold. Had her bed out on the porch. It was freezing cold.

So I asked the nurse, I said, "What do you do, why do you all have her out there in the cold like that?"

She says, "Look under the cover and you'll find out."

And I did, and the maggots was—Oh, my God. Oh, my God.

So I brought her home, because she wouldn't sign the papers. So there wasn't nothing they could do.

I brought her home, and the lady told me, she said, "You get some calimer powder, and just put it on there, just as much as you can, just keep putting it on until it's caked on there."

And I did.

And the foot healed up. It did. It healed up for a while.

But then we had to have special shoes made for her, for that foot, you know. But in the end, she lost that foot; they had to take it off.

Aunt Effie lived right up the street. This was her sister, but she'd just gotten married about six months ago. And I had been taking care of Aunt Eliza and didn't know what it was to go out.

I asked Aunt Effie one day, I said, "Aunt Effie, there is a program that's gonna be on to the church, and I have never heard of this man. This man's name is Father Divine, and I have never heard of him. I've heard *of* him, but I've never *heard*, you know—"

She says, "Well, I'm sorry," she says, "but I'm having guests and Mr. Hamilton wouldn't approve of it."

I said, "What did you say?"

She says, "I'm sorry, I'm having guests and Mr. Hamilton wouldn't approve."

"So you mean to tell me you can't take off one day and take care of your sister."

"Not today."

"All right, Aunt Effie, thank you very much."

So I said to my husband, "You go ahead. I'll stay here with my aunt and take care of her. You go ahead."

That was on a Thursday. Friday I went around and I looked for a place. I couldn't find any. You know what I did Saturday? I had the moving man to come out to the house and move every stitch of furniture that my aunt had—every bit—which there was a lot of antiques, which was silver that belonged to me that she had given to me. Moved every bit of it up there.

She cried out—what was her new husband gonna say?

And I said, "Well, isn't that just too bad." And I left her there. "This is your sister. She's my aunt. I've been taking care of her for five years and the least that you can do is to help. I don't know what it is to go out on a date with my husband." I said, "I don't have a chance to go anyplace. My husband and I haven't been to a movie in two years, together. And he's fed up with it. And so am I." I said, "She's your sister. At least you could come down and stay with her a little while."

So I left her there. Of course, I'm not gonna tell you that I was happy about it.

My husband said, "Now the best thing to do—pack up, leave right here."

I said, "Why . . . what?"

"Leave," he said. "Let's go to Philadelphia."

Aunt Eliza also moves to Father Divine's kingdom.

I have to laugh when I think about this. You wanted to know if I had ever seen Father Divine. Yes, I saw him. They threw me out of his church. It was in a small building on Fulton Street in Brooklyn, with homemade benches.

I wanted to see for myself because the people were saying that he was God, and I had to see this man. So I went with my Aunt Eliza.

He was a little short baldheaded man, I mean his head was clean. His wife was blond—he married a white woman. I never saw so many diamonds on a person in my life, because she was loaded. And when they come in—the chairs up on the pulpit of the church, they were painted gold—and when they came in, when he come in, they put down this red carpet for him. And he had this long cape on, and two fools in the back holding the hem of the cape to keep it from dragging on the floor; and when he would go up, he would just undo it and let it fall, and they'd have to pick it up, see. I couldn't get over that. So these people really think he is

God. That's all you could hear in the church: Father Divine is God, Father Divine is God. Well, I got tickled. And they carried on so as if this man was God. They kneeled down and worshipped him, and I just went to pieces. I got so tickled. So they put me out, because I couldn't stop laughing. And my aunt could have killed me. But I got a kick out of it.

I went to visit some of his hotels because I had heard so much about it, about these hotels. I was told that they were spotless. The restaurants were spotless; he had restaurants all over. He bought up a lot of property in New York—I mean in Philadelphia and New York. And this man had—I think it was in *Life* magazine before they went out of business—they showed these beautiful mansions that he had, these beautiful places, abroad, and they said he didn't pay any income tax and the government didn't have any way of making him pay. They don't know how he got out of paying it, but he didn't pay it.

Well, the hotels were spotless, the kitchens were spotless. And people would go there. Now, I used to buy his ice cream, I really did buy his ice cream, but I never ate in the restaurants, but I've seen people eating there, and what they got for twenty-five or thirty-five cents, it would be enough to feed four people. You got all you wanted to eat for thirty-five or forty cents, fifty cents—I don't think there was anything up higher than fifty. You got all you could eat. As I say, I never ate anything there, but I would go in and buy ice cream.

And I remember when he bought the Lorraine Hotel in Philadelphia. Three men, three men came over with suitcases, with the cash—with the cash—to pay for a hotel. I don't know where he got the money from—well, I do know where he got the money from, because my Aunt Eliza took everything that she had left. And Aunt Effie had thirty-five hundred dollars' worth of insurance on Aunt Eliza, because I paid for half of it each month. So Aunt Eliza came and asked for her insurance policy, and Aunt Effie said . . . asked her what she wanted with it. She said, "I want them. I want to see my insurance policy." Well, Aunt Effie didn't want to give it to her because she said maybe she was going to change them. If anything would happen to her, *she* would have the burial. But she raised so much Cain, Aunt Effie had to give her her insurance policy. She said she wanted to look at them. And she took those insurance and turned them over to Father Divine. Well, Aunt Effie told me that she had took the policies. I said, "Well, now look, we have to find out what she did with those policies. Because I'm not going to bury her." I said, "I have taken care of her for God knows how long and I'm not going to bury her." Aunt Effie says, "Well, we'll call her and ask her." So we did. She gave them to Father Divine. So Aunt Effie said to her, "Well, if you took your insurance policies and Erma and I have been paying for them for the last four years, and give them to Father Divine—you get out. You go live with Father Divine." She said, "Let him take care of you and feed you." I said, "Well, I might as well not send another cent. That's it. If you can give him your insurance policies." I says, "I'm not sending no money over here to feed you any more. I mean it."

So she left. They had this place that was called a Kingdom. She left and went with Father Divine. And all of those people there—they were brainwashed. Just like this group of people that committed suicide, they were brainwashed—Reverend Jones I think the man's name was.

Anyway, you took everything that you possessed. If you had a home, you sold it, or you gave the deeds to him. And he and his wife lived like kings and queens. He had a limousine, a chauffeur to drive him around in it. Stupid, ignorant people, grown people, educated people—there was white people that would donate hundreds of thousands of dollars to him. Well, what they did—this was during the Depression—he would take the people off of the street and *feed* them. And they just . . . they said he was God. And some of those stupid people actually believed he was God.

Yes, I've seen him. I'll never forget being thrown out of the church. That's all right—I got a kick out of it.

Managing well during the Depression while others commit suicide.

We came to Philadelphia, to his brother. He had seven brothers up there, all in Philadelphia. And we was here in Philadelphia about two weeks. I got a good job. We had a very good job. All I had to do was rent apartments. A man by the name of Bodick—I think that's how it's spelled. They was very wealthy Jews. They had a gorgeous place in Atlantic City. And after I worked there for about three months they told me, they said, "Erma, you take care of the place, you rent the place, you be sure they sign a lease now, and you collect the rent, and we'll come in once in a while." And that's what I did, and we stayed there for about eight years. And we made good money. We didn't have to pay any rent.

Now, this is during the Depression, this is during the Depression when the bottom had dropped out of everything and people was jumping out of windows and committing suicide. And we stayed there and stayed there and stayed there. There was three suicides committed, and the last one, I smelled this gas. On Sunday mornings we used to take the paper up, you know, and put it to each door. This was out in Upper Darby. Wealthy Jews lived out there. And the last suicide that I walked in on, this man had— I was delivering the Sunday paper to each door and I smelled this gas, and it smelled strong, early in the morning. I thought, My God. So I knocked on the door and I didn't get any answer. I knocked again. I didn't get any answer. I took the passkey and opened the door. And there he was—buck-naked, on the sofa!

Well, I had to run out. So I ran next door, knocked on three or four doors. I didn't know what to do. For someone to please help me turn off the gas stove and everything. They didn't do it. They closed the doors. Said, "Call the police. And an ambulance." And we did. And they came, and they went on in there with their masks on, gas masks on. He had each window stuffed with cotton, and the stove, the oven and the other four burners wide open. He had lost every cent he had.

I said, "This is it. Now this is it. Uh-uh. I can't stay here any longer." I told Mr. Bodick, I said, "Mr. Bodick, I'm sorry but I can't stay here." So we left there. We moved to 1400 North 18th Street, and I think I stayed there for about seven or eight years.

After we quit, I went to work for Mrs. A. J. Newman. Her husband was the president of Phillies Cigars on Ninth Avenue. A. Joseph Newman. I worked there for a while.

Now, these people were millionaires, but the apartment in town, it was very plainly furnished. Everything in there was good furniture, it was the best; everything was, well, I should say antiques. Yes, from the living room suite on up, from the dining room on to the living room and the bedrooms and the library—antique. All the rugs on the floor were Orientals, and all of the draperies—the material for the draperies, I'm quite sure it came from India or Hong Kong, a place like that—

they were custom-made. They were all velvet. Even in the bedrooms, everything was antique.

And about the cigars that Mr. Newman smoked, they were Phillies, but I think these were specials. They were the fat kind. I know they were big fat cigars, and I loved to open that door because the house always smelled so good with the cigars.

I have never worked for anyone that I didn't have conversations with. And I talked with Mr. Newman more than I did Mrs. Newman. And he, when he got home, when Mr. Newman got home in the evening, he wanted to know . . . we would carry on conversations, well, what was going on in the world. Well, I eat that up, and he knew I liked it, and he enjoyed talking about those things. We always did. A lot of times, when I would get through serving, he would tell me, "Erma, sit down while we're having our dessert so we can talk." See, because Mrs. Newman was hard of hearing, and in those days they didn't have little light hearing aids like they do now, like they have them now with the earrings, a little tiny thing that goes in the ear or behind the ear, little small things. Those days they had those great big old heavy things about the size of a tape recorder—larger, yeah, about the size, but thicker, and these wires. She just refused to use it. But me, she could read my lips. But she stayed to herself most of the time.

They had a beautiful home in the country, all kind of fruit trees, swimming pool. They were older people. They didn't have much children, a few friends that came to the apartment in the city. I've been around these kind of people all my life.

And out to the ranch—this beautiful place that they had out in the country, going towards the Poconos.

They were, oh, I think he was about fifty-six, she was about sixty, maybe sixty-two. Kinda heavy. And when he came home, only thing he wanted was his cigar, which I got for him, and his beer and the paper. And no one dare call after he came home. The phone didn't ring. And she would go in her room and read the paper or finish reading a book or what she was reading. He would stay in the living room and read.

*Erma lives in another spotless environment, the
Italian section.*

Philadelphia. Was it like New York? No. The people in
Philadelphia, oh, they're much more friendly. They're more
Southern. At least they will say good morning and good eve-
ning to you.

The homes are even different. In Philadelphia they have
these little small porches—no, not porches, steps. And everybody would try and outscrub the other, to keep them snow-
white. I loved that. It reminded me of Yamacraw.

And I loved to go in an Italian neighborhood, they were spotless. You didn't have to see an Italian to know where you
were—just the houses, the streets. You know, they didn't even
wait for the trash man to come by and sweep the streets. They
did it themselves.

And I also liked to go to their markets, which was out in
the street. This market that they had—all kind of fresh vegetables, all kind of fruit.

The Italians, you knew they were in the street before you
saw them.

I didn't go through the Italian neighborhood. I *lived* there. I was the only black person that lived on that block. I lived next to a family by the name of Paulini, and they were spotless. I've never went into any house in that neighborhood that you couldn't eat off the floor. And we all . . . I did too—I kept my part of where I lived clean, spotless. I got out there and swept sidewalks, scrubbed them down with a broom and rinsed them off with a hose. And the steps were as white as snow. And you see, the Italian women, most Italian women —I don't know what they do nowadays—they didn't work those days. They stayed home, raised their children and kept their home, and one would try and outdo the other to see who could keep the house and the sidewalks and things the cleanest.

And the best wine you ever had in your life. Of course, I had to learn how to drink that wine because it was sour. I had to get used to it. It was made in every house. In the cellar was where the wine was made—every house had it. They had wine every night with their dinner. So I know a lot about the Italians.

I used to make their own sauce and sell it to them. I would. I used to sell it by the quart, because some of the ladies, they played cards a lot, and that sauce was something that they made every day. And if they didn't have time to make that sauce, I would sell it. I used to make it by the gallons and sell it.

All of them were dark, all of them, and most of them were kinda heavy. And that's on account of the pastry, you know, the macaroni and all that stuff—they had that every day, God save. Every day they had spaghetti of some kind. And some of them are real beautiful, some of the women are just beautiful. And the men also.

Through one of Aunt Eliza's old friends, Erma and her sister are reunited.

My other sister—I was two years older than her. She died last year—1976. Catherine, Catherine Young. She married a man, a native of Hilton Head. She would never tell you her age. She was about fifteen when she married.

We used to pass for twins, although I was two years older than her.

Now we were separated. I didn't know where she was and she didn't know where I was. Raised by different people altogether. When my father took me, somebody else took her. I didn't know where she was, and when—oh, I think I was about twenty-six or twenty-seven years old and I was working at the Long Lane Court Apartments. This was during the Depression. But during the Depression I lived better than I ever lived in my life. I didn't know what it was meant by "Depression." Because I took care of this apartment house for these wealthy Jewish people—Long Lane Court Apartments.

And this lady and I was talking.

This lady's name—she's dead now—lady by the name of Miss Ella. She's dead, God bless her.

My aunt had a beauty shop, and that's how I met *her.* And every time she'd come there, she'd say, she'd look at me, she said, "Well, you've got a twin somewhere, honey." And she kept on talking about this thing.

She was over to my aunt's house almost every day. They were very, very dear friends. This is the aunt that disappeared. She left and went to this Father Divine business and we haven't seen her in years. We don't even know where she is. That's my mother's oldest sister.

Miss Ella said, "You look like a girl that I know in Savannah. I'm telling you," she says, "you could pass for sisters." And she kept telling me and kept telling me.

So I was telling her about this sister that I hadn't seen in all of these years.

She says, "Wait a minute. This girl is telling me the same thing. This girl has told me the same story that you've told me." She said, "You know, I believe that's your sister." She said, "It has to be, because you look like twins."

I said no. I said, "I've looked so many years. I'll never find her."

She says, "Let me call her and find out." And she called her.

And *she* called me back.

She says, "Was your mother named Laura Best?"
I said yes.
She said, "Is your name Erma Elizabeth?"
I said, "Is your name Catherine Loretta?"
She said, "You're my *sister!*"

And I sent her a navy-blue—they had started wearing the red boots then—navy-blue dress and the little red short coat and the red boots and the navy-blue hat, so I would know her when I seen her. So when she came, I had on the same outfit that she had on.

But she came to the house. I had to go to work that morning. So my husband went down to meet her.

I said, "You can't miss her, because you'll see the outfit that she has on." He said he didn't need the outfit, but he saw her and he said, "There's Erma." We even *walked* alike.

So when I came into the house she said, "Are you my sister?"

I said yes.

She said, "I thought you would be a great big tall woman."

My mother was tall.

I said, "I thought you would be tall too."

So we looked at each other like, well, like total strangers. We didn't even shake hands. We didn't do anything. We just stood there looking at each other. And we began to talk about things that we did when we were little, and things that we got spanked for, and the tricks that she pulled on me, you know, when we were little. She always was a little devil, and could always beat me. I was two years older than her, but she could always give me a good licking. So all of a sudden she looked at me and I looked at her, and we both started crying, and we hugged and kissed each other, and I'm telling you, it was on.

And she stayed with me. She told me about this fellow that she was engaged to. And she stayed with me about three weeks, and she was just heartbroken. She wanted to see him. So I sent for him.

He was just old enough to enlist, to go into the service. So he did. He went overseas; he was over there for four years. She stayed with me. And when he came back, I went with them to get married. And when he came back, from overseas, they stayed in Philadelphia for a while, and they came on back to Savannah.

She told me that she'd lived on Thirty-sixth Street with a lady by the name of Mrs. King. We were from different fathers. She stayed with her father and Mrs. King. But I didn't know anything about it. I didn't know where she was. She didn't know where I was. Same mother, different fathers.

But you see, my sister would never work. She has never worked. That was out of the question. She wouldn't work.

I got her a job, and I told her that if she went to work, you know, I would help her get on her feet, and save some. But she was getting her compensation from her husband overseas.

And you remember these old-fashioned trunks that they used to have, the top kinda round-like? Well, there was one around on Ridge Avenue. She wanted that trunk so bad. I wanted it too because it was an old antique. She says, "If you buy that trunk for me," she says, "I'll go to work."

I had a job right next door for her. I gets the trunk. And when I came home the next day, my sister was gone: her, trunk, and every stitch of clothes I had but one blouse and a skirt—that's all I had.

I didn't bother with her for about seven years. I didn't have anything to do with her any more for about seven years. You see, it makes a difference when you're not raised together. There's something lost.

So we finally made up, but after we got older.

She came to Philadelphia. Oh, she told me where she went with the trunk, but she had to send for me to borrow four hundred dollars right away. She was in some kind of trouble. I sent it. I did send it. But I didn't bother with her any more for about seven years.

And she came back to Philadelphia and was living right across the street from me. She'd been over there about a month or so, and I used to see this lady pass: Well, gee, that woman looks like my . . . looks like Catherine.

So one day I was in the store.

She said, "Hi."

I said, "Where did you come from?"

She said, "I've been watching you going and coming for over a month." She said, "I live right across the street."

I says, "Well, I'll be doggone."

So we made up.

And she and her husband separated for five years, and he had four boys with another woman, and the woman turned out to be no good at all. So the law took the children away from her and gave them to him. And she wasn't even allowed to even go near the children.

So my sister—he asked my sister would she take him back.

She said, "I will—to raise the children."

She loved children. She took him back, and she raised those children. And you couldn't tell that they weren't her children if you didn't know that she was not the mother. You couldn't tell. She raised those children, and every one went to college but one, and that's because he didn't want to go. Every one has turned out to be something, but one. And when she died, I think those children, part of them, died too. She was dead about . . . I think about three months, and he married her best friend. So I don't bother with them any more.

Catherine tells Erma where her son is.

My sister said to me one day, "Isn't there anything in the world that you want, that you really care for?"

I said, "Catherine, the only thing in the world that I ever wanted, that I ever cared for, was taken away from me," I said, "and when that happened—"

She said, "Fourteen years ago."

I said, "Well, how did you . . . what do you mean, what are you talking about?"

She says, "Your son."

I said, "Well, how did you know about my son? Who told you?"

She says, "I know where your son is."

I said, "What!"

She says, "I know where he is."

I said, "I don't believe you."

She says, "He's in Savannah, Georgia."

I said, "Well, how long have you been knowing this?"

She said, "About a year."

I said, "Oh, my God."

She says, "But you will have to be a woman." She said, "I wouldn't want him to see you like you are now. You . . . you still haven't grown up." She says, "You are going to have to be a woman. And you're gonna have to learn to stand on your feet and act like a woman, and I'll see that you see your son."

Well, of course, you know what happened to me, I went to pieces. I did. But I did as she told me. I went out the next week that I got paid. I bought my own clothes. I went to the beauty shop. And when I saw myself I didn't believe it. This can't be the same person. It's like a child getting ready for, oh, a Christmas, a birthday party—no, more than that, more than that.

But I'll tell anybody. I don't care if it's a child, if it's an adult. The worst thing in the world to do is to kidnap somebody. Because when you kidnap a baby from its mother, you're not only hurting that baby, you're hurting the mother and the father. They are going through a life of hell, because that's what I went through. Every time I saw a woman pushing a carriage, I would scream. That's right. I don't believe in capital punishment, but anyone . . . if it's kidnap—yes. Yes. Because I think it's one of the *cruelest* things in the world. Because God, and only God in heaven, knows what I went through for fourteen years not knowing whether my son was alive or dead.

When he was born he had gray eyes—bluish gray. And no one could understand, though—where is this little brown-skinned baby with these blue-gray eyes? Brown-skinned children doesn't have eyes that color. Yet they were gorgeous. Well, I found out later and I think you found out later, and you will find out later when you meet some of my relatives where these eyes came from.

My sister took me down with her to Savannah, and we went to this woman's house. She knew who I was when I walked in. She knew exactly who I was.

So I said to her, "I came to get my son."

She said, "Well, he's not here." She says, "And another thing—you are going to pay me every day for the fourteen years that I kept him."

I said, "I'm not going to pay you anything because you didn't keep the child. You *stole* him. So I don't see why I have to pay you one cent."

She says, "Well, you'll get him over my dead body."

A friend of my sister's, a woman named May, brought him over that afternoon, picked him up after school. My son was in the morning class. They used to go to school half a day, a class in the morning and one in the evening. He was in the morning class.

All right, when the child came in, there was four other boys with him. They were all looking like little ragamuffins.

And my sister said to me, "Now, you said you would know him."

I went over to him and I put my arms around him and I said, "Hi, sweetheart, I'm your mother."

He says, "You're my mother!?"

"Yes, darling, I'm your mother."

I knew him. I knew him by those eyes. I just knew him. Isn't that something? But I knew him.

Miss Pearl showed up the same night. My son was still there.

A man came upstairs, a friend of hers, and told me that Miss Pearl was downstairs and wanted to see me.

I didn't care if she wanted to see me. Catherine didn't want me to go down there. My son stayed upstairs.

She was outside. She got out of this truck. Two other women were in there with her. And she pulled this gun on me and she said, "You call him and tell him we're going."

I saw the gun. Pointed at me. Right then I was so mad I didn't care if she shot. I was fighting for my child.

I told her to go. I said, "You're not taking him. And don't look for him tomorrow because I'm going to take him downtown and buy him some clothes."

She finally put the gun down. She let it drop to her side. This man told her, "You're the one that's going to end up in jail."

She says, "Well, I'll go with you."

I said, "Well, it doesn't make any difference if you go with me or not, I'm still gonna take him down and buy him some clothes. And I don't think I want you to go. I'll bring him back."

She says, "You better—"

I said, "I'll bring him back."

It was about four o'clock in the evening.

And he looked at me—he couldn't keep his eyes off me, and I couldn't keep my eyes off of him. He was crying, and I was crying. We cried. My sister was crying too.

So I took him down. Those days they had the open trolleys in Savannah. They were yellow. And if it rained, God help you. And they also had hacks—you know, with the horses. They were called, I don't know, I would say they were like the stagecoaches that they had in the South, in Texas, but we called them hacks.

First place I went and got his hair cut. Took him in, and I bought him two suits of clothes. Oh, about a dozen pair of changing underwear and socks and bought him three pair of shoes. And shirts. And he wasn't used to wearing shoes, and the shoes hurt his feet. But they were his size, and I wouldn't get him any larger.

I said, "You'll get used to them."

I bought him bedroom shoes. I bought him pajamas. And he didn't know what the pajamas were. He thought he could wear them to school. I said, "No, son, you sleep in these. You don't wear them to school."

So I went, took him back, and she saw him, she says, "Well, aren't you a great big young man today! Don't you look wonderful today."

So I told her, I says, "I'm gonna take him back with me to my sister's house."

She says, "How long you gonna be here?"

I says, "For about a week, and I would like to keep him with me for the week."

She says, "All right." She said, "But I'll tell you something. Don't ever come back down here again," she says, "and start any trouble with this child."

So I told her, "I may as well be frank with you. If I have to go to the Supreme Court, I'm gonna get my son. Because I thought he was dead. I didn't know where he was. I searched all of these years for him."

So I asked my sister about the lady, you know, that had told her.

She said, "Honey, she's dead."

I said, "My God, I wished I could meet her." I said, "I remember her, she didn't have any teeth at all."

She said, "She never . . . she *still* didn't have any teeth."

In the week's time I saw my lawyer. As soon as I got back to Philadelphia, he said to me, "No trouble at all. No trouble at all. If she kidnapped the child, *you* can prosecute *her*."

I says, "Well, I don't want to do that. But the only thing I hate this woman for—she treated him *exactly* as she treated me." I said, "He looked like a motherless child, like a little ragamuffin." I says, "How much do you think—"

He said, "You don't have to pay her anything. You don't have to pay her anything."

But before I had a chance to go down, my doorbell rang one morning, about five days after I was home, and there stood my son. There stood my son. He ran away. I said, "Well, where did you get the money?"

He said, "Aunt Catherine gave it to me."

Do you know that he wasn't up here about a month— I had him in school and everything—she came. Of course, her husband was dead; he'd been dead for years. They used to call him Papa Yellow because he was so black that they didn't know anything else to call him, so they called him Papa Yellow.

And she wanted him. She wanted her son. I told her, "You have no son."

So I said, "I'll tell you what I'll do. I won't treat you the way you treated me." I said, "I know you haven't been a good mother to the child, because he looked like a tramp. You treated him exactly like you treated me. But there has to be *some* feeling there. You've been with the child, you've had him all of these years, so there has to be some kind of feeling. Let him tell you *whom* does he want to stay with. If he wants to stay with you—I've been without him all these years— knowing that he's alive, I'll be willing to give him up. But if he wants to stay with me . . ."

She says, "Well, if he wants to stay with you, then you can have him."

"All right, we'll do that."

So he came home from school about three o'clock. And he says to her, "Oh! What are you doing here?"

She said, "I came to get you."

He says, "No way! Never!" He says, "You lied to me all of my life, telling me that you was my mother. I knew you wasn't. I knew it was something different. It *had* to be something different."

She said, "Well, James, wasn't I always good to you?"

He says, "No, ma'am. No, ma'am." He says, "I was the only child that couldn't go to Sunday School because I didn't have shoes to wear." He says, "And I was the only child that went to school with no shoes on. No, ma'am, you was never good to me."

"So you don't want to go back with me?"

"No way. Not unless my mother don't want me. Not unless my mother make me go."

I says, "Honey, you don't ever have to go back with her, or anywhere, *any*where. Anything that you don't want to have to do anywhere in your lifetime, you don't have to do it." So I said, "Now are you satisfied?"

He told her, "If I go back, I'm not going to stay with you. I know where my real mother is, and I know this is my mother, because I can feel her love. I can feel it." He said, "You never gave me a bath."

She says, "She gave you a bath and you're fourteen years old?"

He said, "I wouldn't care if I was nineteen. Yes, my mother gave me a bath."

Huh! Oh, God bless him. God bless him.

So she says, "Well, will you promise me this?"

I said, "Yes?"

She says, "Will you bring him back to visit me?"

"Well, I'll not only bring him back," I said, "if he wants to come back and visit you, I'll give him the money. He can come and visit you. I'll do that."

She says, "Can I tell you something else?"

I said, "What?"

She says, "I'm so sorry. I can't say that I'm sorry," she says, "because God knows I love the child. I love the child."

I said, "You had a helluva way of proving it, though. You treated him exactly as you treated me. He told me he slept on a little cot—in a room full of junk with just a little cot. He was lucky, I said, because I slept behind the counter on croker sacks, and I didn't know what shoes were either, or clean clothes. The only difference, he didn't have to steal his food to eat like I did. You remember all those things? You remember?"

And my son jumped up. He said, "You treated my mother like that way?"

I said, "You keep out of this now. Now, you sit down and just keep out of this."

She said, "Well, I didn't know any better," she says. "I was always jealous," she says, "because I never had children of—"

I said, "That was no excuse. My mother fed you. You was one of my mother's best friends." I said, "I should have stayed with my father, because it couldn't have been any worse. It couldn't have been any worse. Only thing," I said, "they stayed on me, they beat me for breakfast, dinner and supper. But you—you was worse. You was worse." I said, "But you got paid back. Because you've had him all of these years. Now he's a young man, and you really need him because you're old. And I have him. So, you see, revenge is for God. Now how do you feel?"

She says, "Just let him come to see me. That's all I ask."

I said, "All right." I said, "I'll show you that I . . . I've shown to you and proved to you that I'm more of a lady than you are," I said, "because when I was in Savannah, you pulled a pistol on me about my own son."

"Yes, yes," she says, "I'm all alone now, I have nobody."

I said, "Oh, you have somebody."

"Who?"

"You have a lot of memories to think about, and they're all bad. I have to get my supper ready because my son and I, we're going out." I said, "I'm taking him to a place that he has never seen—had never seen in his life."

She said, "What is that?"

I said, "He has never seen a ballet. That's where I'm taking him."

She said, "Well, what is that?"

I said, "Well, it's a little bit too late for you to find out what things like that are. It doesn't concern you any more."

*Erma joins the war effort building ships, and
separates from her husband.*

Now the war had started. And the pastors, the ministers in
the church, would get up and beg all able-bodied women,
everybody that can do anything—go! They had schools to
teach you how to weld, welding, because we were short of
men.

And the pastor used to get up in the church every Sunday
and talk about—"We don't have the ships. We don't have the
submarines. We don't have the planes. We have to get somebody out there. The men are gone. Who's going to do this?
It's up to you women."

And so I joined. I went to school and learned how to
tap and weld. I went for six months. Some of the women just
went for three months, but they had to go in as tappers, but
I went in as a welder. And then when you get over there you
had to take a test. I was so nervous, but I passed. I went to the
shipyard in New Jersey.

So I went. And then we used to wear big old heavy thick
men's shoes—you know, for safety. Dungarees, khaki shirts,
old hats.

I rode the buses and the subways and the trains. Because when I worked to the shipyard, I had to get the trolley, then the subway, which went over the river from Philadelphia to Jersey, then a bus. I worked from twelve to eight in the morning. I loved that. I did a lot of crocheting while I was riding.

When you're building a ship, you start from the . . . just like you make a dress pattern—you have the patterns, right? You got the blueprints of the ship, and it starts on the bottom. It starts on the ground. And they can take that steel and bend that steel any way they want to, and when they get that steel bent, you have to weld it, so it'll stay that way. You build your ship from the ground up.

That's why I have arthritis right now, laying out there on that cold steel in the wintertime. The river froze. I mean the river was solid. You could walk on it.

And I made good money. You better believe it.

And I worked at night, I worked the night shift. This time Catherine was living with me. I had to hire somebody to come in and do the cleaning because she wouldn't do anything. She wouldn't do it.

I was working the night shift, and one night I came home because I'd had a flash, and you know what a flash does to your eyes when you're welding. So they brought me home.

And my husband wasn't there. He didn't come in until five o'clock the next morning. He didn't even know I was in there. He went on in the kitchen, got himself something to eat, changed his clothes, his good clothes he hung them up, got his work clothes, and went on. He didn't even know I was home.

So I said to my sister, "How long has this been going on?"
She says, "Ever since you've been working."
I said, "I don't believe it."
She says, "Yes."

So I found out that he was having an affair, and found out who the woman was. She'd call up there.

Of course, I tried to die at first—but, no, I don't think I really . . . I never loved him, to be frank with you, because I knew nothing about love. I didn't know anything about love all of my life until I met Tony. I didn't know anything about it.

So we separated. As a matter of fact, I put him out. Because he had never bought me a chair, not one chair. Everything that I had, I bought myself. All the furniture I bought myself.

So I put him out, and when he went out, when he left, I kept on working. And I accumulated enough money to buy a house.

Jack and I had been separated for about . . . I've forgotten now how many years. I was on my own and doing okay, working hard, doing the same thing that I did before. Working hard, coming home and going to church.

Oh, I think I worked on that for about a year. I got so many flashes I had to stop.

Erma's son, James, enlists and goes off on the train with about twenty other neighborhood boys.

My son and I stayed together—God bless his soul—until the war started. And he enlisted, and went in.

He volunteered. He and twenty boys left the neighborhood. They all left that same time. I'll never forget watching that train go out of sight. I thought I would die. All the parents that was down there with their children was crying.

And I thought that that train looked like the longest, biggest . . . I don't know, it just looked to me . . . I watched it until it was out of sight. And I cried; most everybody did—oh, everybody, all the mothers, the fathers that was down there seeing their children off, they cried. My son enlisted. And he left for the service the same time—the same day that my husband and I separated, my son left that evening. So for the first time in my life I was alone.

But I got used to it. I did. I liked it. I liked being alone. At least I had peace of mind.

He was overseas for four years. I wrote him every week, sometimes twice or three times a week, and sometimes he would get them all at one time.

There wasn't a week that I didn't send him a box. Every week I sent him something. Not only did I send *him* boxes. I sent boxes to each one of those boys. Each week I'd send a box to somebody. Every week I sent packages. I made cookies, candy, homemade candy. Just like I did when they were home. They always stayed to my place for ice cream and cookies and things, and I didn't forget them. But it was sad for them not to come back.

And I used to stop and think, Well, my God, why me? Why? Now I just found him, I just got him. Why? Why take him now? And please bring him back to me. And I prayed so hard for God to please bring him back, and He did. He came back with not a scratch on him. He was in the Philippines, and he was in Germany, and several other places over there, but he came back without a scratch. The funny part of it was, he was right in there with the thick of it, fighting— not a scratch. He says that he knew that there was someone praying for him. The fellows told him, "Adderley, someone's praying for you. You have a guardian angel somewhere, because you should have been blown to pieces with the rest of the guys." He says, "Yes, I have a guardian angel—my mother." He says, "Because I'm gonna see my mother again" —which he did.

I thought he was lost once. I couldn't . . . no trace of him. They couldn't find him. But he was blown off of that—you remember they blew up that bridge, the bridge in Germany. It even blew his dog tag off. He survived. He didn't know where he was, and they didn't know who he was.

But he was lost; I don't know how he lost his dog tag, but he was lost. And they didn't know where he was.

I couldn't find him. I kept writing and writing and writing and going to the Red Cross, and asking, you know, had they located him yet.

I used to go to the Red Cross every day. That woman got so sick of me that one day she couldn't stand it. She said,

"I'm so sick of you coming in here every day. The same question. You're not the only one that has somebody that's serving."

Before she knew anything, I had reached over there and grabbed her by her neck. I said, "Don't you think that I want to know whether my son is living or dead? That's the only child I have."

And the other nurse to her, the other lady told her, "You've got a nerve. If she comes in here *fifty* times a day, you don't have no right talking to her like that. Do you have anybody in there?"

"No."

She says, "Well, all right, then."

But they finally—well, he had that . . . amnesia.

Finally I got this letter that he had been found. Oh, that was a living hell. That's right, I went through a living hell then, but thank God, he came back. He and Johnny and Butch.

When he went to the service, there was twenty—they all went in together, all friends. When they came back, only three came back alive. One had lost an arm. One had lost a leg. My son didn't have a scratch on him.

And you know, those days when the boys came back, the whole neighborhood would be decorated, and we'd have banners all across the street from one part of the house to another—WELCOME HOME—and their names on it. That's right. And we'd have big parties, big block parties for the boys that came back alive.

Erma's son marries.

When my son came back home, he married a girl by the name of Ethel Fisher. And the first baby's name was Erma Elizabeth. And the second little girl, they named her Hazel after my daughter-in-law's mother. And I think the third one was James. I don't whether there's six—I don't know how many there is now—because I lost track of them when I went to Mexico and came back. I have been trying to find them ever since, but they are in Philadelphia.

Not him—I know he's dead. I found that out, that he was dead. But I would love so much to see my grandchildren, and one day I'm going to find them. I'm going to find them. Erma Adderley, Hazel Adderley, Ethel Adderley, James Jr. Adderley. If there's any more, I don't know anything about them, but I'm going to find my grandchildren if it's the last thing I do. When I came back from Mexico, as I said, I lost track of them.

He died of cancer. He's been dead now for about four years.

Erma plays pinochle and goes out to the ball game.

As far as the baseball—I *loved* it! I never missed when Jackie Robinson played.

Who took me to the baseball games? Oh, I went with so many people. All you have to do is say, "Let's go." And I loved it.

Not just one person, I went with so many people— friends, people that I knew in my church, we would go. We ladies, there was about six of us—no, twelve, there was twelve that belonged to one club. We played pinochle. And there was nobody in Philadelphia those days who could beat me playing pinochle. I *lived* on it. I loved to play it. Now, I wouldn't know how to make a . . . I wouldn't know how to start it.

And we ladies used to go. They used to have something they called Ladies Day. It was cheaper, you know. That day was Ladies Day. And what stopped me from going—Jackie Robinson, that was my favorite, he hit a home run. And I was sitting next to this Italian woman.

And he was going through hell those days. He was really going through hell.

The bases were loaded.

I said, "Jackie, put it in the bleachers. Do that for me. Please put it in the bleachers."

And this Italian woman told me to shut up.

I said, "I paid my money to get in here just like you did. You're saying what you want to say to the pitcher, and I can say what I want to say to Jackie. Put it in the damn bleachers, Jackie! Put it in the bleachers!"

And that's exactly what he did.

She jumped up and slapped me! Well, I was shocked. And what the hell she hit me for? I reached up and pulled her by her long hair and her and I—oh, we had it. We fought like two tigers.

So her husband said to her, "Are you crazy?"

"Officer! I want this woman arrested!"

He said to her, "*You're* gonna be arrested." He said, "You hit her first."

Well, we were both excited.

So I said, "No more ball game. No more ball game." I've never been back to the ball game.

About Roy Campanella, I remember him. He and Jackie, they were something. They were *something*. I admired him. I remember this man, he was something. He and Jackie Robinson.

*Erma goes to Mexico with Felipe Asoto-Esparza to
get married, and escapes before the wedding.*

Yes, I went to Mexico and stayed there a year and a half. I
was going to get married. I changed my mind once I got
down there. I changed my mind.

Felipe Asoto-Esparza. I met him in America. He used to
work for the Pennsylvania Railroad. And we were engaged
to get married, and I wrote his parents, and she wanted us to
come over there to get married.

I used to come down and visit my sister. And I had a very
dear friend—her name was Esmiamara. She was from the
Virgin Islands. I took a trip with her, to her home, and we
visited Puerto Rico. Well, I've been about most every place.
I've been to Louisiana, I've been to—oh, well, I've done a lot
of traveling.

And I had read so much about Mexico.

So I told Esmi about two weeks after that, I said, "Esmi,
I think I'm going to Mexico. You look after the house and
take care of everything for me."

She said, "Of course."

So we went.

I got me a book to try to, you know, find out what English meant and what it meant in Spanish. And I didn't do so bad. I could go and shop. And I learned that they would try and cheat you. I learned *that*—that was the first thing I learned about the money.

The funniest thing about it, these people had never . . . most of them had never seen a black person before in their life. This was a little small place by the name of Condella, and these were Mexican Indians. And they were the nicest people I've ever met in my life. They were just so wonderful to me. They brought me chickens, they brought me pigeons, squabs, rabbits. I even had them to bring me goats. And they'd bring me cheese, which I wouldn't eat because I didn't know . . . But one family that I met, they were spotless, and that's where I got my milk from, my goat milk. And I love it today. It was hard for me to drink at first, but I love it today. I wished I had some now. And you know, in Mexico the coffeepot was going all day long. And that's where I learned how to make tortillas and chili and cook Mexican dishes. I learned that from those people.

And I stayed a year and a half instead of a year. I really did.

I loved Mexico. I loved the people. But not in the city, not the big cities. You don't know anything about Mexico if you're going to Mexico City or some of the big places like that, you don't know anything. But you go in the little small villages and you meet the people. They're wonderful people. I didn't want to come back.

And this little town, Condella, was deserted. Anyone moved into any house they wanted because there was no work there and most of the people had gone.

They had baked beans and tortillas. And anything . . . they didn't have much more. No work. The only work that I knew was they grew their food, taking it to the next town to sell for just a few pesos. Not everyone had meat, but everyone had chicken and they had a few goats. When all of the grass was eaten up they would have to move away from around where they lived. And they took their pigs and the goats. I couldn't understand and I still don't. The little boys would have to—like little shepherds—bring the cattle. And the pigs and the chickens and the children and the wife was packed in, piled in the wagon.

And they had like the thing that they made the tortillas on—it's a thick heavy piece of iron that they take it to the blacksmith shop and he pounds it for them. And they just put it on two bricks, because, you know, there's nothing there but bricks and rocks—you don't have to look for that. And they took a lot of flour with them, and lard for the tortillas. Salt pork—as a matter of fact, just fat meat. And plenty of goats—took all their goats because that was really their income. They sold the milk and they also made cheese out of it. The cheese is delicious if you know what house to go to where it's clean. They couldn't afford to butcher the goats, because they needed them for the milk and the cheese and that was an income. And beef was butchered once a week. And the only people that had cows were the two people, the two men, that had the stores. And when they went to buy their meat, they would take a . . . oh, buy a little tiny piece of meat that you could hold in your hand to feed maybe eight or nine people, and you wonder, How in the world are they gonna do it!

But they had their vegetables growing. Everybody had their own vegetables. They would put in onions and garbanzos—it's a bean that they used. Garlic—and they grew their own tomatoes. And it wasn't so bad for them. But I couldn't eat it. And the coffee, well, that boiled all day. You couldn't drink it because it was black and as strong as I don't know what. Because everybody came and you had to have a cup of coffee. You didn't dare refuse.

Their main dish was pinto beans—pinto beans and tortillas and a little chili powder. Very seldom do they have meat to season their food with.

These are the poorest people that I've ever seen in my life. You know that's why they come over here—they'll take a chance and cross that river. They don't care if they're gonna get caught or not.

When they get about, say, they get five pounds of pinto beans, it's three pound of stones in it. When they get through cleaning the beans and picking those little rocks and stones out, they don't have nothing. But you can't do that in this country and get away with it.

I traveled twice. The first time I traveled, it was on a bus. And we were so high up on the mountain. This little road it was just for one car. There was another route for the one that was coming the other way. And it was so high up there, I wanted to get on the other . . . by the seat, to see, to see down, to look down. And when I looked down, the little donkeys looked like little dogs. And then when I looked down a little closer and saw how much space we had, I almost dropped dead.

So the next trip that I took, it was in a wagon. Now, we had to go across this river. And that water—it was a lot of rocks, but they know where to cross—and that water was like suds, just churning. And when we got in the middle of the river, that water was to the bottom of the wagon and I almost dropped dead. I came back in a car! So I didn't do any more traveling then until I left. You know me, when I get scared, nobody can beat me praying.

Most . . . now, I don't know about the cities, but in the small villages you never will find a señorita out alone. Someone's going to be with her. But now in the big cities it's just like it is anywhere else. And when a young man comes calling—you think they're going to leave them alone in the living room or on the porch? No, indeed. Somebody older has to be right in there.

Because in the little villages, the small towns, if a girl marries and she's not a virgin, the husband doesn't have to stay with her. He goes to the priest.

That's what we went over there for, to get married. Got the license and everything when we got there—but uh-uh!

The fellow that I was going to marry, he tore my passport up, see, and I didn't have any way of getting out of Mexico. Because if they catch you without, and you don't have that passport, you can get lost in a Mexican prison, I'll tell you right now. Because if you go in there, you *may* come out. They *may* hear from you again. And I knew that, because I had been reading a lot.

And he tore up my passport.

I think the president then, his name was Lopez. President Lopez. I wrote him and told him what had happened, that I didn't have no passport, and I was an American citizen and I couldn't get out of Mexico. You know, he sent me a passport. He certainly did. I hid the passport. I gave it to—the fellow that I was going to marry, I gave it to his mother. Because he was insanely jealous. If his brother came there and he came home and his brother was sitting on the steps, he'd try to die. I thought, No, this ain't gonna work, no. If a man's jealous of his own brother . . . No, this, no, this ain't gonna work.

I don't think there's anybody in the world any more jealous than the Mexicans.

So he loved to travel. I said, "Let's go to Laredo."

Well, you know, the river separates Texas and Mexico, and there's a bridge. Right in the center there's a gate there, right in the center of that river. And all of these rocks—look like some of them tall as this tree—and this water is so rough, if you fall down there, that's it. Well, anyway, America must claim half of the river, and so does Mexico, because this bridge is right there in the center—the gate is.

So I said to him, "Let's go. Let's go to Laredo."

He said, "Okay."

And his oldest brother, José, and Alicia, his sister— they're in on it. I left all my clothes. I left everything. Guadalupe, his mother, cried for two weeks because she knew I was going.

So when we got there I said, "Let's go over here and see. Can't we go over and talk to the soldier?"

He said, "You're not supposed to."

I said, "Oh, come on. Let's go over to the soldier."

So we went over there, and the American soldier's on this side and the Mexican soldier's on that side of . . . this gate. So I got right up to the gate, and I said to the American soldier, I said, "I want to come through—"

He said, "You an American citizen?"

I said, "Of course I am."

He said, "You got your passport?"

And I reached down in my bosom and I pulled out this passport.

Now—the Mexican soldier, he's pulling me back *this* way, and the American soldier's pulling me back *this* way.

Because he was screaming, "That's my wife!"

I said, "I'm *not* your wife!"

So the American soldier said, "She's an American citizen and she's got a passport and she wants to come back in her country. She's coming back in this country, and nothing you can do—"

And they was pulling me backwards and forwards.

So the American soldier told them, "Okay, you better turn her loose now. Turn her loose."

So they turned me loose.

Boy, I was so glad to get back! Oh! I was so glad to get back in Laredo, Texas, I didn't know what to do. No more Mexico. No more Mexico!

Erma visits her sister again and comes home South.

I stopped by to visit my sister on the way back from Mexico. And I stayed there, I think, about two months. And it was so *quiet* and peaceful. It wasn't nothing but dirt roads, you know. It wasn't like it is now.

And when I went back to Philadelphia I couldn't stand it. It was so wild and crowded and clustered—all of these homes sticked together—and noisy. I just couldn't stand it.

I had a house in Philadelphia, a three-story white house. I told my girlfriend, "Do you want this house?"

Now, Esmi had always been very good to me. Because I had a hysterectomy, an operation, when I was in Philadelphia. She came to see me every day. She took care of my house. When I came home she took care of me. And she always said, "Gee, I wished I had a home, a house, but I will never be able to give a down payment." And I think I owed about . . . I think it was $8,000 more on the home, so I said to her one day, I said, "Esmi, would you like to have this house?"

She says, "What?"

I said, "Would you like to have this house?"

She said, "Would I like to have it? You mean own it?"

I said, "Yes."

She said, "What do you mean?"

I said, "If you want it, you don't mind paying the lawyer to change it over, you can have it."

She says, "Look, are you crazy?"

I said, "Well, do you want the house?"

She said, "Of course!"

I said, "Well, okay, you'll pay the lawyer to exchange it—you know, turn it over in your name—and you've got a house."

She said, "What are you talking about?"

I said, "I'm going back to Hilton Head. I can't stay here. It's too noisy, it's wild. It was bad then with people stealing and breaking in." I said, "I can't stay up here. It's too noisy. And down there," I says, "the beautiful grass and the trees, you hear the birds singing, and the chickens, the rooster crowing in the morning." I missed all of that, you know. I said, "I can't . . . I can't stay up here, I couldn't stay up North any more." I said, "I've had it. I can't live in this city any more. It was nice and quiet in Mexico where I lived, and in Hilton Head," I says, "it's nice and quiet."

I left. Packed my things up and got me a . . . Mayflower, I think was the name of the van. I moved my things down here in my sister's home. She didn't have any furniture.

*Erma finds a job on Pinckney Island and meets
Colonel and Mrs. Edward Starr, the DuPonts
and Mr. and Mrs. James Barker.*

Of course, there was no paved roads there, those days in Hilton Head. There was nothing but dirt roads. And there was two trucks on the island—that was all, because they had to come in by ferry. Nobody owned any cars. And there was two white families on the island. There was *only two white families.* That whole island once was owned by blacks, and they sold it for twenty dollars an acre or a hundred dollars an acre. Now you have to pay sixty-five thousand dollars down at Sea Pine to get—it's not an *acre*—a *lot.* They gave it away.

So I stayed down with my sister, and one day the manager came over and asked me would I—did I know anyone that could cook, wait on tables. I'd never done anything like that—worked in a restaurant—I know that.

So I said, "Well, I'm going to be frank with you, yes, I think I could do it."

He says, "Someone that knows how to make salads and desserts and things."

I said, "Yeah, I could do it."

He said, "Well, come on over and try anyway."

I said, "Well, all right, when do you want me to start?"
He said, "You can go now."
I said, "Now?"
He said, "Yeah."
I said, "I don't have any uniform."
He said, "We have uniforms to fit all sizes."
That was about nine o'clock in the morning.
So I went on over there. I went to work for Pinckney Island.

Before you get to Hilton Head—when you leave Bluffton—the island is the first island you come to after leaving Bluffton. The road that leads to Hilton Head, you have to cross over Pinckney Island before you get to Hilton Head. When you leave Bluffton there's a bridge, which is solid, you know. Then, the Barkers and the Starrs gave the government a piece of the island to go across. If they didn't give it to them, they would have condemned it anyway, so they gave it to them. And you cross Pinckney Island, then you come to the drawbridge that you have to open for the shrimp boats and all of these big yachts to cross.

And there are seven islands. They lived on the main island, which is, I think, about seven miles long. That's where we lived. About the island being like just a dirt road, that's the way they wanted it. That's the way they enjoyed it. It's the most beautiful thing you've ever seen in your life. You see, these people go to all these fancy places all over the world, and they want something that's quiet and different.

And this island was privately owned. You couldn't come in there. There was no way to get in there. You had to have . . . the people that worked there, we had keys. Not everybody that worked there. I had a key and Tony had a key and the Smiths and her husband, they had a key. But nobody else.

When I first went to Pinckney Island, I did the salads and waited on the tables.

They had a girl there to do the cooking. So one day she was sick, very sick, and they had to take her home. The Barkers weren't there then. The Starrs were there. See, this place belonged to the Barkers and the Starrs. And I had heard so much about the Barkers, how mean they were—oh, they were the worst people in the world.

So anyway, I went, I cooked dinner.

I think the Rockefellers . . . no, not the Rockefellers, the DuPonts were there.

And after dinner Colonel Starr and Mrs. Starr came into the kitchen and said, "Erma, this is the first decent meal we've had since we've been on this island." She said, "We've never had homemade soup. We've never had homemade hot bread. And I've *never* tasted venison cooked like this before in my life."

I said, "Well, thank you."

So then she wrote Mrs. Barker and told Mrs. Barker, she says, "We've got a girl that is over there now that is terrific."

Then I met the Barkers—I said, "Oh, my God, the Barkers are coming."

And when the Barkers came they had dinners with the Starrs and then they would leave the island—the Starrs would leave—and the Barkers would stay with their . . . have *their* guests.

The Barkers' guests were the Rockefellers, General Doolittle, the Fords. You know, each had their own group.

When the guests came, some stayed for two weeks, some stayed for a week or some stayed for two or three days. And when one group would go, you had to get ready for the other group. But you see, the groceries was bought—we'd go out and buy about six thousand dollars' worth of food. Eggs was bought by the crate.

We bought eggs by the crate. You had to. Eggs and all kind of soups, Campbell's soups, all kinds, all kinds, buy fifteen to twenty-eight cans of each kind—that's until I started to making homemade soup, and that was it. No more canned soup.

On the island everything was bought in large quantities, because to get back from the road to the island to the clubhouse was over six miles, and no one could come out there two and three times a day, or every day. Of course, they had to come out every day to go to get the mail, but that was right across in Bluffton. But there were lots of things we couldn't get in Bluffton. You had to go off certain places to get it, you know, in Savannah. When the club would open, that's when most of the stuff was bought. But you still had to keep going until the hunting season was over. So everything was bought in large quantities. It's not like being in the city and you can just go to the store. It wasn't like that.

And then you have to stop to think about, as I say, these were the same people that came every year, year in, year out until they just passed away. And you knew what everybody wanted, so you had to have a lot of different stuff in there for these people. So, therefore, everything was bought in large quantities. And nothing came—no desserts or sweets came—from the store. They ate a lot of grapefruit; now, the grapefruit were bought by the crates. Not the oranges, but the grapefruits were. And although they ate a lot of grapefruits—they had grapefruit every morning, sometime they had grapefruit for night. . . We usually had grapefruit for night when the Barkers were there alone. The Starrs didn't have desserts, only when they had guests. But all the cakes and all the pies and all the cookies and all that stuff, I had to make it. Mr. Barker was very fond of my pound cake. And I've forgotten now who loved chocolate cake, but everybody liked something different. So therefore we had to have everything on hand. There was all kind of different sauces you had to make, and there was all kind of . . . my salads, I like to dress my salads up and I just didn't like lettuce and tomatoes or tossed salads. I like fancy salads and I loved fancy desserts. And therefore we had everything on that island that anybody needed.

And I'll tell you something. If you don't know it, I do. Rich people—they have a *circle* around them and they don't associate with anybody else. It's like a clan, it's just for them, nobody else. They don't want to be bothered when it comes to entertaining or giving parties, or having friends to their house. It's for certain people, and they just don't bother with other people. And the same people that have been coming down to the island for years—they came every year. They were invited six months or so ahead of time, and that was a privilege to them, you know, to be invited down to the island.

On Pinckney Island, the same thing was done over and over each year. The same people came. The same meal was cooked for each guest. They wanted the same thing when they came, and I knew what each guest wanted.

And each one that came, I knew what they wanted. Each one wanted something different. Now, there was the Rockefellers. Mr. Rockefeller, he loved spoon bread. Mrs. Rockefeller loved oyster stew. *He* didn't like the oyster stew, but he loved the gravy off of it, the soup off of it. Mr. Knopf, well, when he came down I didn't know what he liked, but I made him—him and Mrs. Knopf—noodle pudding. And they enjoyed it.

You know, they were the last ones that came on the island, they were the last guests. After Mr. Barker died they were the last ones. And when they left there, they knew they would never see Mrs. Barker again. They knew that.

And there was one lady there that loved apple pie for breakfast in the morning. You don't believe me, do you? That's right.

And at first there was no telephones on the island, because, as I say, they didn't want to be bothered. They didn't want no phone calls. They wanted to be left alone. That was it! Oh, the police department had one, in case anything happened, you know, we could call them and they would come there right away. Not only that, they had to have it—when General Doolittle came down, he had contact with the White House. That's the only time that the cops would come, I think—yes, to bring a telegram, to give him a message. As I said, that's the way they wanted it. They wanted it strictly private.

And the guests—another reason they wanted their privacy, they didn't have to be all dressed up. They were sick of that. They had it all their lives. They could come down there dressed any way they wanted to. But at night for dinner, *everyone* got dressed for dinner. That was the law in that house. At that club. This was a private club for the Starrs and the Barkers and their friends.

And you know, they never invited new friends. There was never any newcomers. They came until they died. And finally they died out one after another, until there was nobody left but Mrs. Barker and Tony and I.

After their death they gave the island to Wildlife.

So when I went to work there, I *stayed* there. Otherwise, you had to come over every day in a boat. And sometime that water would be rough. And they really couldn't get anybody to stay over there.

And then, from cooking, I just took over the job of being the manager. That was it. I did all—made all of my grocery lists out. And after I married Tony, I sent Tony to the store. He did the shopping. And Tony kept, like, the wood and things in there for the fireplace. And things that had to be done around there that a man could do—he did it. So we just stayed there and took care of it.

And that's how I met the Barkers. And so many wonderful people that I've met *with* the Barkers. I worked there for twenty-five years.

Erma meets Mrs. James Doolittle, Mrs. Helen Knopf and Mrs. James S. Rockefeller.

Mrs. DuPont and Mrs. Knopf—I think they're the only two ladies that ever came on the island that didn't hunt. Oh no— Mrs. Doolittle, she didn't hunt either. Mrs. Doolittle would fix the prettiest centerpieces and flowers. She arranged the flowers so beautiful, and Mrs. Rockefeller did too. Very, very pretty. Whenever they came we always looked forward to them decorating.

It was two cemeteries over there. Slaves . . . all black, you know—one for the slaves and one for the soldiers.

I can show you the cemeteries where the First World War . . . the old veterans that was buried there. Some of the graves have sunken in.

You know, years ago when people died—the black people—they put their favorite shaving mug or their cups or fancy dishes on the grave. I went out there and took off and brought them home. I *did* so. And I have plants in them. Mrs. Rockefeller took one mug home with her.

*Erma always has plenty to do on the island and on
the water.*

In the summer there was always something to do. I cleaned
my house every morning. I had a garden. I had beautiful
flowers. And I put up vegetables for the club in the summer.
I remember one summer I put up four hundred quarts of
tomatoes alone. The Barkers loved figs. I had to put those up.
And I made cookies by the dozens, and they were frozen. Because Mr. Barker loved cookies. And I made soup—all different kind of soups, every kind of soup that you can name—
and that was frozen. And I went fishing every day if I could
get a chance, but as I say, while the vegetables and fruit was
fresh and plentiful, that's what I did.

And I would go up to the club with Tony when he went
to work in the morning and work up there—until he worked
off and come home—canning. And as I say, we had homemade soup twice a day—for lunch that was the first course,
and the first course for dinner at night. Well, I wasn't idle.

I was very happy there. And Tony and I would go into
Savannah for a movie once in a while.

And you know I'd rather stay there than go to Savannah.

When I went to Savannah, I was like a fish out of water. You saw all kind of beautiful trees. All kind of animals. You sit right there and see two and three hundred wild turkeys on the parade ground in the front of the club. You sit there in the front of the dining room—there was all this *huge* glass, just all this beautiful glass—and look out on the marsh. You could go out there and get all the marsh hens you wanted. Tony used to go out there and get the biggest fish that you ever saw. That was paradise. It was really paradise. And you would really have to be . . . you really would have to be a person that would hunt and love nature to understand why these people kept coming back.

You know, I lived in every house on that island but the manager's house that the Smiths lived in. That's right.

I wished I was over there now. I really do.

And up on Boat Point where I lived, I loved that better than any place I lived. Because we would see these beautiful ships, these gorgeous yachts. Sometimes they would come up if the tide was high. We've even had them to come in when there was storms and take them in until it was over.

And I lived at the boathouse. I loved it there too, because I could walk out of the house and walk right on the rock and fish all day. I loved it there. But when I had to go to the gatehouse, I couldn't stand it. Because there was no privacy. The minute you would sit down to eat, somebody . . . you'd hear a horn blowing and you have to go out there and see who it was, and I locked the door.

And about it being dark at night, you better believe it. Now, at the time when I lived over there, there was no light even at the gate—but now they have one there. Wildlife has put up a light by the gatehouse where I lived. Three—they have three lights up there now. They're getting it ready. They're working on it now, for the public, you know. I think that property was worth five million dollars if I'm not mistaken. I think so.

I imagine it sounds dull about Pinckney Island, but it

wasn't dull to me. But as I said before, you would have to love nature to love this place. But it's a beautiful island. Beautiful palm trees. And you wonder, well, why do these people keep coming. They come back because they loved it. They *loved* it. The same as we did. I was in such a hurry I wanted to come home and stay in my little house. But you know something? I wish to God that I could go back. I don't think I could stand it without Mr. and Mrs. Barker, though. No. Tony said he never wants to see it again.

Erma visits friends across the river, and the Smiths.

Oh, and about me going across the river in that boat! That
was a little old bateau that the men used to pick their oysters
in, to put their oysters in. These little boats are rather flat and
they stay on that . . . they have to stay until the tide comes
up, after they get the oysters in there. The water was eighty
feet deep, but I didn't know it then, I didn't know it that
time. The water was choppy, but you know, when I get in
trouble nobody can beat me praying.

I was just in a little bateau. I didn't realize how deep it
was, and I didn't know that . . . you see, the wake, it can
get rough out there in a second. And we had plenty of sharks
down there. You better believe it. Never went back any more.
God was with me.

And why I went across this river, there was a friend of
mine sent me notice that day, "Come on over." She had something for me. Because the first time she sent for me, she had
this great big sunfish. That thing was almost as long as this
table, and thick. I mean big around. Beautiful. I made steaks

out of it. They'd never seen one like it; they wouldn't eat it. It was beautiful. Sunfish.

So the next time I went over, she sent word for me to come on over, she had something for me. And I went. And what do you think she had for me? This great big beautiful piece of meat—I never saw nothing so pretty before in my life.

I said, "Well, what kind . . . what kind of meat is that?"

She says, "That's gator tail."

I said, "No, ma'am, not for me. No way."

She says, "Well, we got three, and I thought maybe . . ."

"No, *ma'am*."

She said, "Have you ever . . ."

"Nope. Never tasted . . ."

"You don't know what you're missing."

"Well, that's all right, I don't wanta know. I don't want no parts of that. No way. No!"

Talking about taking the boat over the river to the island, I did that twice. The fellow that took me that lived over there on the island, Dan, he could handle a boat. But I didn't know until the second time that I'd went across that river and back—we was living on the island at the time, I was, but Mr. Smith, that was June Smith's husband (they were the managers when we first went there), he told me about somebody drowning. I think there was two or three people that drowned out there.

I says, "What!"

He said, "You know that water's eighty feet deep?"

I said, "You're kidding me?"

He said, "No I'm not."

It was rough. It took about a half-hour to go and a half an hour to come back. I never did it any more after that, after I found out about these people drowning. So I asked his wife, June, about it the next day.

* * *

Their son, Randy Smith—now, when he came home from . . . when she came home from the hospital—he was born while they was on the island also—when they came home from the hospital with this baby, she handed him to me. And I was the first and the only person, I think, that ever spanked him. Nobody. Because when the Smiths brought him home, Mr. Smith let us know, "Don't touch Randy." And Randy knew that nobody couldn't spank him. But I tore him up. I tore him up. Oh yes. And when I did, I snatched him out of his father's lap to do it. He did something he had no business doing, and he ran and got into his father's lap and I snatched him up and tore him up. So Mr. Smith wanted to know what it was.

That boy got mad with me because I wouldn't stop my work and give him some ice cream, and he was big enough he went in there and got ice cream anytime he wanted it. And when Mr. Smith saw what Randy . . . Which he went in there and put the hose on twenty starched white shirts that I had ironed for Mr. Smith; I had them hanging up on the bathroom on the shower curtain, on the rod. And Randy went in there and got the hose and opened the window and turned it on the shirts. I tried to kill him. And when I turned him loose, and told Mr. Smith, he said, "What do you mean by spanking him?" He said, "Nobody's supposed to spank Randy." I said, "That's the trouble. He's six or seven years old now, and he's never been spanked in his life and nobody can't do anything with him." I said, "He runs the house, but he's not going to run me." And he said, "Well, what you. . . anytime he do anything you tell me." I said, "What good does that do? You go in there and see what I spanked him for."

And he went in there and he saw the shirts. He grabbed him. And I had to get in between him and Randy, because he . . . I thought he was gonna kill him that day. And from then on, he told me anytime he does anything that's wrong, he said, "You got my permission to spank him. Put it on him." And I stayed on him for a while. And he knew that I would, you know, tear him up. So we didn't have no more trouble with the young man.

When I'd go home, they'd call me. Sometimes when I got in the house, off the job, I'd hear the phone ringing. It'd take about twelve minutes to get up there—about fifteen minutes to get from down there, the gate.

And I heard, "Hello. Randy been this—"

I said, "I'll be right back."

He'd get on the phone. "Please don't come down here. I'm going to bed right now. I'm going to take my bath and going to bed."

"Okay."

And that was one of the baddest little things you ever saw, because he was spoiled. But not now.

The Smiths had a daughter, too, Alice Smith. When Alice was six years old, I don't think there was a man could beat her shooting. That's right. She could handle a pistol and a rifle like any ranger, and she still can, can handle them both the same way. That was the manager's daughter. That's the one that she and I went to the cemetery and stole all of those things off the graves. That girl was the girl that was there when I went fishing in a boat and the boat went over.

*Erma, now with a house on the mainland during
the Pinckney Island off season, meets Tony
Calderon from Puerto Rico.*

Tony couldn't speak one word of English, and they took him
to the hospital. He wouldn't let them touch him.

So Dr. Gatts, he sent for me.

He said, "Erma, you know the little Puerto Rican?"

He lived by himself.

I said, "Yeah." And I couldn't stand him. I couldn't
stand him—because he wouldn't speak to nobody. Not knowing that the poor man couldn't speak English.

So he said, "Erma, will you please go to the hospital and
talk to that man?"

So I went there. And I talked to him. He was laying up
there. He was in the room with another white fellow. I went
out and bought him pajamas. I bought him a razor. I bought
him magazines. And a carton of cigarettes.

He told the man. He said that when I walked out the
door, he said, "Well, I'm gonna *marry* that woman."

But I didn't know anything about this, see.

So when it was time for him to come home, Dr. Gatts

said, "That man can't go home by himself. Somebody has to help him."

So Mrs. Smith said, "Well, he can't stay here because I have a young daughter."

He said, "Well, what's wrong with Erma? She's got that great big house down there by herself. Let him go—"

I said, "No way, no way. No, sir."

So he said, "Well, Erma, you know, you can lock his room off from your part of the house at night."

So that's what I did.

And I took care of him.

So he stayed there, and I took care of him, and when he got well, I said, "Now you have to go back home." I said, "You can't stay here with me."

He said, "Go back home—where?" He said, "You want to marry me!"

I said, "I can't marry you," I said, "because there's too much difference in our age, Tony."

And I . . . he wouldn't take no for an answer.

But it worked out all right. So far.

The wildlife of the island: snakes, alligators and wildcats.

When I first went on that island, I didn't realize what was there. They have these great big huge wildcats. They have alligators. And you know, God was with me because I would *walk* from the club over to the house where I lived, all the way up to Bull Point, at night, with just a little flashlight. But I wouldn't do it now.

I used to walk that island up and down—at *night*. And I didn't know that rattlesnakes crawled at night. When it's hot, they try to stay in a cool place. But God must . . . God was with me. I have never been bitten. I have never seen one at night.

And one day Mr. Barker—ha!—brought the claws of this wildcat home, and I saw it. That did it. No more walking the island at night—or day. I would walk from the club to the manager's house, which wasn't very far—about, oh, it'd take you about five minutes to get there. And I was deathly afraid, because I found out that the chicken snakes stayed up in the trees. One day I was going there and one fell right in the front of me, and that was it. So we had one of these old-fashioned telephones there in the club—remember, you crank it up—and it was just for the island, not on the outside. So whenever I wanted to go down there, I would call June and tell her to come and get me or to bring me such-and-such a thing. As far as walking? No, sir. I lived on that island all those years, twenty-five years, but the last five years—I was afraid.

*Erma falls in love with the Barkers, and listens to
radio opera with Mr. Barker.*

Well, when I met Mr. Barker . . . the first time I saw Mr.
and Mrs. Barker I fell in love with them. Right away!

Mr. Barker was a remarkable man. He had a brilliant
mind.

There was no such a thing as no right and wrong. It
was one way. That was the right way.

Never . . . I have never given that man one glass of
water that he didn't say, "Erma, thank you so much, you are
so good to us."

He was a gentleman, so help me, he was one.

And Mr. Barker and I—ohh! Every Saturday we got the opera
on Pinckney Island. Nothing interfered with that. Nothing!
Not on Saturdays. The only thing that ever interfered with
our opera on Saturdays was when Betty and Bob was coming
to visit. But other than that, we had our opera every Saturday,
because that was the only time you could get it on radio and
no one else down there was interested in it. *I* hadn't found

anyone. But Betty sent me one of the most beautiful records, and I love it, I played it to death. I love it.

About the opera. I saw *Othello*, and that was the only one that I'd ever seen. All the other ones was what I heard on the radio. Because down here you don't get opera. You don't get it on the radio but only on Saturdays.

*Mr. Barker extracts a promise from Erma, and
wills her a legacy.*

Before Mr. Barker died, when we were on the island, before
we went to Chicago, he said to me one day, he called me,
"Erma."

I said, "Yes, Mr. Barker."

He says, "If I die today or tomorrow," he says, "would
you take care of Mrs. Barker?"

I said, "Now, Mr. Barker, you didn't have to ask me
that. You know I will."

He said, "You really will take care of her?"

I said, "Of course I will."

He says, "I don't want her put away in no place, no
home. I don't care how exclusive they are, how fancy they
are. I want you to take care of her. You promise me?"

I promised him.

When he got ready to go to Chicago (I was up there
with him once) when he found out . . . They found out
down here that he had cancer and they wanted him to go back
to see his doctors in Chicago.

And I told him I wasn't going. I said, "I am not going back up to Chicago." I says, "Mr. Barker, you can hire anybody you want, any kind of person."

He started to crying. That man sat to that desk and cried like a three-year-old baby. Then *she* started. Then *I* started. Tony started. The little dog, Tinkerbelle—her picture's all over the album—Tinker: *Aaaoooooooooh!*

I said, "Now, this settles it. This settles it."

He says, "Erma, go ahead—how much more do you owe on your house?"

I said, "I owe thirteen thousand dollars more on it."

He said, "Well, you bring your deeds in here to me."

Do you know, he paid for it? He paid for it. That's right. And he left me a fifty-thousand-dollar trust fund. I get the interest off of that—live off of that.

All right, when we went to Chicago, he would send Tony and the nurse and Mrs. Barker out when he wanted to talk to me. They knew it—they better go because he was going to talk to me.

"Erma."

"Yes, Mr. Barker."

He'd set down and talk to me and tell me things he wouldn't tell his own children.

He says, "You know what you promised me?"

I said, "I'll keep my promise." I said, "As long as I live she will never go in a home. So don't worry about that."

And I kept that promise, too. I kept it.

Back to the island.

Of course, when Mr. Barker died, we went back down there.

So when he died, she says to me, "Let's go home."

They had this gorgeous place up there, beautiful place, but she didn't want to stay there. And I can understand, because there was too much there. But when we got on the island, it was the same thing. There was a lot there to remind her of him.

We used to go over to the little cottage where they lived. They didn't live in the club. They had this small little tiny cottage. Here were these people with all this money in the world, and wanted to live as humble as they could, and that's the way they lived. And *I* called it the "love cottage," because there was so much love there, between them. You never saw two people so close—they were one. They loved each other so much. It was a beautiful thing to watch.

After he died and we came back, Mrs. Barker would say to me, every day, "Let's go to the little cottage, Erma."

And we would go over there, and you could almost *see*

him, *feel* his presence there. Everything was just like it was, you know, when they were living.

Before he died, they moved over to the guest house—before Mr. Barker died. And that night I had to move again. Because then I occupied the suite of rooms that the DuPonts had. Here I was in the Big House. And it was beautiful there, just gorgeous.

Tony—he stayed there for a while. He would go to Bluffton. He had to get away. He'd go over there and he'd stay over there a couple of hours, and he'd come back. And a lot of times there was nobody on the island but just Mrs. Barker and I. And I would be petrified—but she wouldn't know it—until Tony came back. The gate was always locked —but Tony had to get his shotgun. And we could see from the club: boats landing on the island, and people getting out with rifles—you could see them, we used the glasses. And he would go out there. I said, "Oh, my God, these people all have guns, because you can see it from here. Now he's going out there, with a gun and a pistol. They'll kill him." But nothing ever happened. He just told them it was private property, they couldn't hunt there. So they'd walk away, they'd go away.

And we used to go out there and in about twenty minutes we'd have a whole bushel of clams. On Pinckney Island. I will always love that place, always, as long as I live. But to be there without Mr. and Mrs. Barker—I couldn't. I just couldn't.

*Don't let anyone tell you that there ain't no such
thing as ghosts.*

So many people that I've known since I worked on the island
have passed away.

And you know, one night Mrs. Barker came down to
my room, she says, "What do you want?"

I said, "What do you *mean* what do I want?" I didn't
want anything. "What do you . . . what's the matter, Mrs.
Barker?"

She said, "Well, you knocked on my door."

I says, "No I didn't."

She says, *"You knocked on my door."*

I says, "Mrs. Barker, I didn't knock on your door."

She said, "Well, *some*body knocked on the door, and I
said come in."

I said, "Well, it wasn't me, because you know I just put
you to bed." I said, "Maybe you was dreaming."

She said, "You just *left* there, so how could I be dreaming? I couldn't go to bed, you know, to sleep that fast."

Every night it was the same thing.

So one night I was putting her to bed—and I heard someone *knock on the door.*

And she says, "It's not *you* because you're here. So," she says, "come on in, Tony. Tony, come on in."

I said, "Mrs. Barker, Tony's in his bed fast asleep."

She said, "Well, it *has* to be Tony."

I said, "No it isn't."

So I opened the door and there was no one there.

She says, "Let's go to the little house, Erma."

I said, "Well, have you heard this before?"

She said, "Yes. And every time I tell them to come in— they *don't* come in."

And *don't* you let anyone tell you that there ain't no such thing as ghosts. That's a lie. There *is.*

I was going through the living room, to the kitchen, one day, and I saw Mr. Barker stretched out on the same couch where he always stretched out.

I didn't say anything to anyone.

And I wasn't afraid. It didn't frighten me.

About three weeks after that—the *same thing.*

I says to myself, Now, you know, somebody has to go. Either he has to go, or *I'm* going.

But I never mentioned it to anyone—until now.

One day she was so upset—one night—I don't know what was wrong. She wanted me to come in there and sleep with her. And I did.

I slept in Mr. Barker's bed, and I heard someone say, "Uh-hew"—that's what he used to do, you know. He had a habit, if I served his dessert, something that he liked very much, he would say, "Uh-hew."

I opened my eyes and there he stood.

I didn't say one word. I just looked at him, put my head

under the covers, and when I took my head from under the covers—he was *gone*.

Then I told Tony. I said, "I'm scared to death."

He says, "What of? *That* can't hurt you—that's just a spirit."

I said, "Well, *I* thought there was no such a thing as ghosts!"

He said, "Well, now you know better?"

Yes I do. I know better.

I've never said anything to her. But she said to me when we moved over here, "Nobody knocks on my door any more. Don't nobody knock on my door any more."

I said, "That was your imagination."

She says, "What about the night that *you* was in there?"

I said, "That was *my* imagination."

But I know better. I know better.

"You're my daughter."

Let me tell you something. Mrs. Barker was so fussy about her clothes. You don't put no blue dress on her and pink shoes or white shoes. You're going to put blue shoes on her. Fussy about her clothes. And sit there! I had to comb her hair three times a day for her, and she'd sit there and primp. And her jewelry. Oh, God bless her!

And sometimes she'd have an accident, you know, and she would say, "Oh, Erma," she said, "I hate you have to clean up after me like that."

I said, "If you say that to me one more time . . ." I said, "You know, you don't have no pants on, I'm going to spank you!"

Then she'd laugh.

But I'll tell you one thing. I don't think anybody in the world has ever been told that "I love you" as much as she told me. And one day when she was so sick, she held her little arms out to me, she says, "My daughter."

I said, "Mrs. Barker, Cecily's all the way in California."

"Uh-uh. I'm talking about my daughter—you! *You're* my daughter."

That's the first time she said that I was her daughter. Well, you know how I felt! Well, I just went to pieces.

And I never went anywhere or she never went anywhere that we didn't kiss each other goodbye—I don't care where it was.

I loved that woman. I couldn't help from loving her. There wasn't a day pass when she didn't say to me, "I love you." There wasn't a day pass. That's right.

And then she'd tell me, she'd hold her little hands out, she says, "My daughter. You're my daughter."

So how could I help from loving her?

Oh, I'll tell you something. When she died I almost died too, right along with her.

Now, when Mr. Barker died, it hurt me. Naturally, it hurt me. But you see, Tony was more with Mr. Barker. He took care of Mr. Barker, you know. Well, Mrs. Barker and I, we were like . . . Oh, well.

But I'll bet I'll never love nobody else like that no more. I will never let myself get involved like that with anybody else, ever.

Erma sings for Mrs. Barker.

Mrs. Barker would say to me every night, just like you would turn on the radio, "Sing. One song. Just the chorus. Sing."

And like you would sing to a baby and it would go to sleep, that's what she did.

> *"How great Thou art,*
> *How great Thou art."*

Then:

> *"How great Thou art,*
> *How great Thou art."*

That was her favorite song. Every night.

The last time I sang it, the whole family was there, and it was all I could do to sing it.

I told Bob, I said, "Bob, I can't."

And—"Erma."

And I tried. I sang it.

Sometime I would reach a high C for her. When I sang it like that, she opened her eyes—and I thought, Oh, I know what she wants:

> "*How great Thou art,*
> *How great* Thou art."

And she closed her eyes.
Oh, Lord!

Mrs. Barker moves into Erma's house on the mainland.

I didn't show you the little bed that Mr. Barker made. That's the bed she died in. She wanted that bed brought from the island, and I brought it over.

I had beautiful white bedroom furniture—I had to get rid of it. Because she wanted her books. So I had to give all of my furniture away. I did everything that she wanted. Everything that she wanted, we did it.

Oh, my God. You know, I hate to talk about her. I don't mean that I hate to talk about her, but . . . It never leaves me. There isn't a day pass . . . there's not one day pass that I don't think about her. As a matter of fact, I don't think she's ever left me. That's the way I feel—I don't think she's ever left me. I think she's around me all the time. I feel it. I can feel her presence.

Sometime I'll say to her, "Okay, I know you're here."

I can feel her presence with me. I don't think she's ever left me.

Erma and Mrs. Barker see The Exorcist *twice.*

Mrs. Barker and I—we were just like this. We even bathed
together, we took our baths together. Oh, Lord! We'd go out
to movies. What was the picture that she wanted to see and
I was scared to death she was going to have a heart attack,
because she'd had three heart attacks? *Exodus?* Is that it? No.
The Exorcist. This is about this child that was possessed with
the devil—you remember? Well, she wanted to see it, and I
didn't want for her going to see that picture because I knew
what was going to happen. So when it was all over, I'm looking
at her—I couldn't watch the picture. You know what she told
me?

I said, "Mrs. Barker, come on, let's go."

"No, we're going to see it again."

I said, "Well, Lord!"

She was a wonderful woman for her age. Wonderful for
her age!

One night we went over to the . . . where they had seafood
dinner. And I called him and told him, said to get us a seat

right by the window so we could see the shrimp boats. So we got this quart of wine. So when the wine was about that much left in the bottle, I says, "Mrs. Barker, let's go."

"What about the wine?"

I said, "Well, we can't carry the wine—that looks bad."

"Well, we'll just order something else and we'll stay here. We're going to drink our wine."

Now, ninety years old! Isn't that sweet!

And she used to tell me, she said, "You know, when I get a little stronger, we're going to take a cruise."

I said, "Where are we going?"

"Anywhere we want to go. We're going to go someplace. You and I and Tony."

I said, "All right."

Erma sings "How Great Thou Art" one last time.

All of the children was to the house Sunday. Mrs. Barker died that next Wednesday, and everybody had left. They all left Sunday. And they were all standing around the bed.

And the doctor had told me, he said, "You, you'll have to go to sleep, Erma." He said, "If you don't, you're gonna die. You're gonna drop dead right on the— Go to bed!" He gave me a pill. I took the pill. I knew it wasn't going to do no good.

So she started hollering, "Erma." All the children were there.

"Erma. Erma!"

The doctor came and got me. He said, "Erma . . ."

I said, "I told you so. I told you so. I couldn't leave her."

So I went there.

She held up her little arms to me. I went on the side of the bed, she put her arms around me and I put my arms around her and she says to me, so weak she could hardly talk, "Sing."

And let me tell you something. I don't know where I

got the . . . I don't know where God gave me the strength to sing that, to sing it, but I sang it. All the children—when I got through everybody was crying. But where I got the strength to sing that song to her—"How Great Thou Art"— I don't know! But I sang it.

And after I got through singing, I started to run. And her granddaughter ran behind me, down the road. And she was so sweet—Beatrice was so sweet. I don't know what I would have done without that child that day.

No, I'll never get over Mrs. Barker. Never.

I'll tell you one thing I'll never do, though, I'll never get wrapped up in nobody else like that any more. I'll never love nobody like that any more. *Never* again.

I lost my son, I lost my mother, I lost Mr. Barker, and right after Mr. Barker died, I lost my sister, but I've never in my life had anything to hurt me as much as this. Never.

Erma makes a final trip north.

When Mr. Barker was cremated, we brought his ashes back here, and I had them there in the house. And she was cremated, and I gave her ashes to the undertaker, and they shipped them up North. And then we had to go for the memorial service. And I stood there at that service, and I (General Doolittle, he was there, and quite a few prominent people) stood there and I looked at those two little urns.

I said, "You mean to tell me that's all that's remained of my Mrs. Barker and my Mr. Barker." And . . . Who took me away? Somebody took me away. I couldn't stay.

I don't think I could ever love anybody as much as I loved that woman. I really don't.

General Doolittle—every time I see his picture in there, I just . . . oh, it just does me so much good. He sent Tony his picture autographed to "My Best Friend, Tony." And he also sent Tony a thing to clean his gun with. Ah, well, God bless him. He came in the kitchen and he told me one day, he said, "Erma, you are the last, you're the last of the Old South."

Erma and the Barker family.

So I don't have anybody now but Tony and my Barker family—I'll always have them.

And Mr. Barker used to tell me, "Erma," he says, "you're not help—you are family."

And you know, that's the way I feel about them. I feel like they're my family. They've always treated me as if I was somebody in their family.

"I've had my share."

I never did go anyplace.

Like today, I don't go anyplace.

Would you believe it if I told you I get up, clean, fix Tony's breakfast, clean, do what I have to do here, fix my lunch—'cause I don't eat breakfast—and get a book. And I'm annoyed if the phone rings. I'm annoyed if anybody comes to the house.

That's what I want. Because I have gotten up at five o'clock in the morning so many years, and stand on my feet until eleven o'clock at night, sometimes a quarter to twelve. I don't want to go anyplace. All I want to do is sit and read. And I'm contented and I'm happy.

Oh, well, I've had my share.

About the Authors

ERMA CALDERON lives in Bluffton, South Carolina, with her husband, Tony.

LEONARD RAY TEEL, an award-winning journalist, has worked on the *Atlanta Journal* since 1969. He is completing his Ph.D. in history at Georgia State University and lives in Atlanta with his wife and son.